CHANGE AGILITY

Leadership, Transformation and the Pursuit of Purpose

A Guidebook for Leaders

KIRAN CHITTA

This book is dedicated to family, friends, clients, colleagues—and, most of all, to my teachers.

Thank you for helping me to pursue my passion and purpose.

ACKNOWLEDGMENTS

This book was born out of a desire to challenge the status quo in the field of "change management" and the various leadership and organization development practices that relate to change. It has benefited from significant editorial input, friendly guidance, and academic oversight from Dr. Ric Roi, who is a leading global thinker and practitioner in leadership and organization development. Ric and I spent long hours sharing our experiences, our sources, and our insights, distilling forty years of collective experience in assisting organizations with the challenge of change.

Organizational change continues to be and will, in our view, forever be one of the critical focal points for all corporate leadership endeavor. We both felt that a practical synthesis and a guide would be more useful to clients than an academic review of current research or case literature. I'd like to take this opportunity to thank Ric for his time as a close friend and collaborator. His wisdom and mentorship as I put together the models and ideas that informed *Change Agility* were instrumental. I'd also like to acknowledge the role that several colleagues and clients I have worked with over the years in different organizations all over the world have played in helping me to formulate the ideas and examples in this book. In fact, this book represents not just my own ideas but an amalgamation of ideas of all those I work with as clients, collaborators and associates at Caxton & Co.

BRIEF FOREWORD

Change agility is the new paradigm for leading transformation in the complex, unpredictable system we know as the multinational organization. The leadership framework and insights offered in this fine book present a holistic and pragmatic approach to change. Using the language of adaptive human systems, the author has presented a way for leaders to solve change dilemmas faced by corporate leaders across all sectors and geographies. For those of you seeking to improve your personal and organizational agility, this book provides an excellent road map with which to get started.

—Dr. Ric Roi, managing director for Asia/Pacific Leadership and Succession Services, Russell Reynolds Associates

PREFACE

Most of us working in global firms have come to the realization that the approach we take to supporting executive and organizational effectiveness needs to evolve. The world we are all living and working in is increasingly unpredictable and volatile. The models of change and leadership that have been taught all over the world, however, can assume far too much control over organizational outcomes, placing too light an emphasis on an appreciation of the impact of complexity and chaos.

Thirty years ago, we might have applied a more mechanistic approach to the design and transformation of large organizations. This is the domain of *change management*, which proved very valuable in a more predictable time. Many of the fundamental practices of change management are still relevant and important for us to adopt. However, today we must also apply an approach that is more suitable for living and dynamic ecosystems. Human systems, including organizations, are all interconnected ecosystems. They are naturally interdependent, capable of self-organizing, sensing both opportunity and threat, responding locally and at the macro level to patterns in their environments, and learning through collective experiences and experimentation. When we study the adaptive, complex systems to be found in nature, we can learn lessons that inform the practice of leadership and organization development.

Change is a paradox. It is both incredibly tough at times and has the potential to keep us truly alive on the inside. Change is my passion. The nature of organizational life in general fascinates me, frustrates me at times, and gives me purpose. I have chosen to think and write about change, while also helping several clients around the world with their change challenges in a consultancy and facilitation capacity. This publication uses the learning from real work, practice oriented research and academic exploration, undertaken in partnership with many others in my professional ecosystem. I have used the editorial 'we' rather than authorial 'I' throughout the rest of this book. This reflects a lengthy process of collecting then sharing, in hopefully a helpful and digestible way, a large body of combined knowledge. Where such knowledge is concerned, arising from a large community of practice, in the words of a founding father of Gestalt psychology, Kurt Koffka, 'the whole is other than the sum of its parts'. I invite you to interrogate the assertions made throughout this book, in the context of your own experience of change, and derive personal insight.

Kiran Chitta, MA (Oxon), MSc, CPsychol, AFBPsS
Managing Director, Caxton & Co., Singapore, 2014

You can't stop the waves, but you can learn to surf.

—Jon Kabat-Zinn

INTRODUCTION TO CHANGE AGILITY

Change agility reflects a shifting paradigm for organizational change. The effective leadership of business transformation or strategy execution has been proven to be a fundamental requirement for successful executives and organizations. Change agility can help leaders thrive in this era of global economic transformation. It is essential in uncertain times for business and government leaders to cope with extremely high levels of ambiguity. Large-scale business transformation efforts often fail to deliver value because leaders sweep complex human realities under the carpet and then try to deal with these realities when it is already too late.

Caxton & Co has put together a leader's guidebook to change that is grounded in both research and professional experience. Complexity is especially clear and present when we deal with real issues in real time rather than in academic research or in classroom training. The real world of work is our learning ground as psychologists and practitioners in organization development. Scientific inquiry and evidence are critical to our work; yet, for the purposes of a leader guide, the science remains behind the scenes. This guidebook is not a detailed presentation of research data or the latest academic theories designed to demonstrate our own expertise and academic rigor. We seek to offer a point of view, a model, and a method for the development of change capability for the busy executive reader. We hope aspects of *Change Agility* are memorable and helpful in your own practice as a leader.

To this end, we have deliberately kept this book short, sharing a practically relevant model for leadership, teamwork, and organization development. The guide is split into three sections. Section 1 covers the "why" of change agility. We briefly explore the context for change agility in today's business environment. We share our views on the landscape of change management practice as it applies to the world we are in. At the end of the section, we provide our own initial definition and description of change agility.

Section 2 then covers the "what" of change agility, going into more depth on the model so you can get a clearer sense of how it could be of use to you. We describe the success factors that underpin the model and the dilemmas that inform change-agile leadership practices.

Section 3 provides our ideas on ways in which change agility creates the basis for leadership, team, and organization development. We share several hints and tips for you to improve your own and your organization's performance, particularly during times of change or transformation. Each section has organizational examples and illustrative cases at its end. We have kept these cases very short and simple just to anchor the model in some real-life scenarios so you can see how it might apply to your own challenges. The examples combine different experiences, and we have used educational license to synthesize them to capture the essence of change agility. All the scenarios are completely anonymous.

The three Rs—reading, 'riting, and 'rithmetic—are no longer enough. We must add the three Cs—computing, critical thinking, and capacity for change.

—Fred Gluck

SECTION 1

THE COMPLEXITY OF ORGANIZATIONAL CHANGE

For most of the executives we work with today, particularly in the largest global multinational organizations (and regardless of hierarchical positions or jobs), reality is that any kind of leadership role, especially within any major transformational change effort, feels like being a Formula One driver. Leadership is living life in the fast lane. You must manage considerable risk, and your own career is possibly on the line. You have personal "skin in the game." Your competitors' actions are hard to predict while you make changes to your own business, and the competitive field is crowded. Unpredictable events can happen at light speed. There is always more information than you can possibly absorb for making decisions about how to shift performance, and yet it is still not enough to give you total confidence in your decisions.

You need to be in control of the process of change, and it is clear that you cannot always be in control. Your business-planning horizon is constantly shrinking. In some industries, such as mobile consumer technology or consumer electronics, serious long-range planning could feel a little academic. All eyes are on you, watching your next move. All that counts, in the end, is your performance: winning. Excuses are not tolerated by your key stakeholders, and you are only as good as your last quarter (or maybe last two). The expectation, also, is that if you do succeed by successfully implementing a winning strategy, you have done so fairly and ethically.

Winning under these conditions takes a huge amount of energy. This guide helps you understand what kind of personal and organizational energy is required for successful leadership in challenging times and provides ideas for maximizing the power of human energy.

Leading Change in a VUCA World

A great deal has already been said and written about the failure rates of large-scale transformational change programs. However, since the global financial crisis of 2008, it is clear that the difficulty associated with strategy execution and change has reached new heights. Around the world, corporate leaders are experiencing something that has always been part of the landscape in military settings: "volatility, uncertainty, complexity, and ambiguity"—also known as VUCA. Many leaders are already familiar with this term.

The meaning of each element of VUCA helps us to understand just how significant it is from a psychological point of view where leading change is concerned.

- *Volatility.* The type of change and the speed of change in business means that transformation is intrinsically volatile.

- *Uncertainty.* The capacity for unpredictable events to hijack the change process required to implement a business strategy is high.

- *Complexity.* Chaos can ensue when we execute on a complex strategy or implement any complex change.

- *Ambiguity.* There is a fog, a lack of visibility, around events and their causes and effects in global business and government, especially when we try to evaluate whether the action we take will actually drive the outcomes we want.

VUCA is the backdrop for change in most modern organizations. VUCA creates serious constraints around our ability to execute strategy and represents the definitive features of any serious transformation effort. For today's organizations, VUCA is a code that implies the need for a permanent state of change readiness.

Examples that illustrate this overarching context are everywhere, across sectors and in all regions of the world. Just take a look at the technology, media, and telecom (TMT) sector. Anyone who works within this sector should relate to the concept that the implementation of transformational change is both a business imperative for survival and subject to VUCA forces. The list of companies who achieved greatness and then fell from grace in this incredibly fast-moving sector is endless—Motorola, Nokia, and Blackberry, to name a few household names that have played, won, and then met serious difficulties in the global mobile devices business. The evidence suggests that these organizations did not have the critical change capabilities needed to achieve sustainable competitive advantages in a crowded, rapidly converging group of industries. Only time will tell now how other firms, like Apple and Samsung, will fare in this regard.

Change agility requires constant vigilance and adaptability. Being number one in any sector is only the starting point for winning—as for many organizations (such as Nokia), being number one is the beginning of their subsequent descent toward relative obscurity. Your challenge is then to redefine the sector, to be a game changer on an ongoing basis, not only to be number one in the world as it is today. Consumers today have a voracious appetite for novelty, quality of experience, and value. Loyalty to a brand in certain industries, such as retail, is also always being tested by competitors. Brand loyalty has been at the heart of the success of many hotel groups, for example. However, with new hospitality concepts constantly being created, especially given the Internet's ability to connect people with an exciting array of accommodation options, even the largest, most traditional hospitality brands can expect to be challenged by new competitors and new business models.

Global hospitality is, indeed, a fiercely competitive sector. If you happen to be a senior leader in an international hospitality group like Starwood, Shangri-La, or InterContinental Hotels Group, you will regularly have to face the challenges of adapting to unforeseen circumstances—like when a typhoon hits a hotel resort or an entire region descends into political turmoil. It is more than likely that even in difficult circumstances, "HQ" still eventually expects you to turn things around and comply with certain global brand standards as part of a global business.

Explanations for underperformance very quickly come across as excuses. The development of a winning culture requires a cadre of high-quality leaders who are able to lead change. These are leaders who can absorb a huge amount of operational pressure, particularly in high-growth regions. They are essential for sustained commercial advantage.

The global financial services sector clearly illustrates the experience of VUCA. Executives in this sector, in global institutions like Citigroup and Royal Bank of Scotland, need to be capable of leading significant global transformation programs. In regional leaders within transforming economies—like OCBC Bank, United Overseas Bank, and DBS Bank in Singapore—executives need to lead their organizations into new territories and markets in order to win. The winners in this sector globally in the next decade will be those who can achieve transformation while also delivering results every quarter. In some of these financial institutions, the nature of transformation in some divisions and regions will need to be comprehensive, touching several aspects of corporate culture, structure, and operations.

Similarly, governments around the world have embarked on hugely challenging journeys of transformational change within their organizations—in the United Kingdom, in several European countries, in various parts of Asia, the Middle East, and across Africa. Each transformational effort has a particular emphasis reflecting the unique public service challenges in each country, but all public service organizations are subject to VUCA forces. The journey for civil service leaders everywhere will not be a straightforward one, especially in serving an increasingly skeptical citizenry around the world that demands and expects better leadership in government. Change, transformation, complexity, and uncertainty are words that really are on the agendas and on the lips of many corporate leaders around the world from Singapore to Silicon Valley.

Historical success rates for change initiatives, however, are not inspiring—as the table below illustrates. Strategy deployment, technological and systems change, restructuring and mergers and acquisitions (M&A), reengineering, and cultural transformation efforts have frequently suffered from significant setbacks. A generous interpretation of the data suggests that there is a roughly 50 percent chance that any serious attempt to bring about major change (or manage change) in a large organization will be successful.

Type of Business Change Initiatives and Reported Success Rates*	
Type of Initiative	*Success Rates Reported by Initiative Leaders*
Strategy Deployment	**60%** average success rate reported
Technology- and System-Driven Change	**35%–40%** success rate suggested by data **28%** large IT initiatives abandoned before completion (Gartner, 2000)
Restructuring and M&A	Frequently involves resource consolidation and headcount reduction to improve operational or cost performance **50%** approximate success rate reported
Reengineering	**40%** estimated success rate using cost reduction as a common measure of success
Cultural Change	Little evidence of sustainable change based on substantial case study literature

*Sources:

- ProSci's 2003 global benchmark study, "Best Practices in Change Management"

- M. E. Smith, "Success Rates for Different Types of Business Change." *Performance Improvement* 41, no. 1 (2002): 26–33. (This is a meta-analysis of forty-nine studies over ten years.)

- R. Roi, *Advanced Change Methodology* (Evantec Corporation, 2003).

Given the sheer volume and complexity of change we believe organizations are dealing with, this success rate needs to increase. It is particularly disturbing that the failure of change often results in unnecessary pain, service failures, and even job losses that might have been averted within organizations. What we do find in today's large corporations, as well as in public sector institutions, is a graveyard of failed change programs and corporate initiatives.

All of the people championing these initiatives had positive, stated intentions at the beginning to deal with new market conditions or to transform the way things were done for positive outcomes. However, it seems that despite a huge amount of academic material and business literature on the subject of organizational change, corporate leaders have yet to master the process of change. This is a failure of both application and the appropriateness of traditional change management methods to help us deal with the level of complexity of modern corporate life.

In the end, employees are subjected to a continuous succession of change programs or corporate initiatives with the usual round of persuasive internal communications, characterized by office poster campaigns and heavily stage-managed presentations orchestrated by human resources and delivered by senior leaders. People at all levels are frequently left feeling quietly cynical about these efforts because they see so many of them losing momentum or being forgotten. This merry-go-round experience many employees have of "visionary leadership," and the resultant changes that actually add little lasting or real value to the business or to the customers they serve, can undermine their overall level of engagement and trust. None of this means that we should give up on change. Clearly, if organizations are not change capable in a VUCA world, then survival can be at stake. What therefore becomes a critical priority is to rethink our approach to leading and managing change so it is more successful more of the time.

From Change Management Methods to Change-Agile Leadership

Within one multibillion-dollar business transformation program at a large retailer, a senior program manager who was working for a technology consulting firm appointed to deliver the change conceded in his own words that "a plan only survives until it meets reality." He was trying to explain why the execution of a myriad of interconnected individual projects and "work streams" was turning out to be so difficult to manage.

The carefully laid-out "technical blueprint" and "road map" created for the program was intended as a tool to help every project team to navigate rather than something the organization could implement in a simple, top-down way. The client's chief information officer, however, wanted certainty and assurances. The CIO was investing the equivalent of around four billion dollars on completely new technology systems across a vast business. The program was clearly too complex for any one person to design in its entirety, to understand fully, or to "manage." The process of change was naturally collective, with ownership for the process widely distributed across a very large delivery organization. This made it tough to control.

The program did yield benefits to the client after years of intense work by thousands of people and extreme levels of ambiguity throughout, although there was some debate around the extent of those benefits at the time. In fact, the actual transformation of this long-established business, after a few decades of underinvestment, took over ten years and did result in a remarkable turnaround in market share, revenue growth, and profitability. This included a complete rebranding exercise and overhaul of the entire customer experience. At no point would this turnaround process, despite a well-structured "program office," have felt like a highly controlled journey from point A to point B. For those involved, the pathway from a state of corporate decline back to market leadership and growth was a human roller coaster requiring agility at all levels.

The role of leaders in shaping and enabling successful transformational change in any complex operational environment is to accelerate the journey toward realizable benefits—to stop the train from derailing and ensure the right people are on the train at every point. The journey, however, is never likely to be smooth or very predictable, especially in a VUCA world. This in itself proved the retailer's program an exceptional personal growth experience for the leaders and project staff.

Comfort with ambiguity and high levels of resilience seemed to be a couple of defining attributes of those who thrived on this journey. Several other direct experiences of large-scale transformation efforts help us reach similar conclusions—in particular that in real life, change is basically messy, far from neatly fitting a straight-line, linear model of project-managed delivery, no matter how hard we try to force it do that. Organizational change generally does not appear to conform to orderly, sequential steps working toward a controllable "end state."

Cloud technology can support transformational change at the speed of light, and big data and software development are very agile; can we also manage organizational change in a more agile way? In the way that cloud technology or agile software development are game changers for information technology services, change agility could be a game changer for business leaders in transforming their organizations.

Traditionally, change management practices have taught leaders to think of the implementation of change as a journey from a current state to a desired future state (that may be several years away). A leader has long been expected to have a grand blueprint for the future, a messianic "vision" that it is his or her duty to both create and hold on behalf of staff. In this model of change, people in general are the recipients of this visionary style of leadership, and the aim of much change management is for them to become willing and enthusiastic participants. The context for this kind of change could be a new global technology platform, organizational restructuring, a merger, a major change in product or in brand, or in culture or service standards. All of these may also require a change in mind-set and behavior at various levels in the organization: a cultural shift.

One of the fundamental features of many popular models for change in current use around the world is the idea that a leader's role is to help people get from the "as-is" state to a "to-be" state. In this paradigm, change is a transition or a transformation from an apparently static, well-understood current state to a supposedly static, easily defined future state. Several change initiatives we have personally experienced tell us that this view of successful change can be helpful and constructive in many ways. However, the actual, lived experience of organizational change for employees and executives all over the world, where hundreds of thousands of people may be involved in several business units across several continents, not to mention customers and external partners, is rather different.

The lived experience of change in today's world is that there is rarely a precise or predictable destination and that change is very dynamic, constant, and multilayered, reflecting the amazing ecosystem that is the modern, global organization. Transformation of a global human ecosystem is perhaps more like attempting to influence any living system than it is to reprogram a computer or rebuild a machine. Natural ecosystems are not easily controlled. In fact, they tend to self-organize. The experience we have is that organizational life today is constantly subject to dynamic forces—at the immediate team level, the geographic level, the departmental or functional level, and at the enterprise level. The agendas at each level overlap and intertwine, creating a tapestry of different changes. Some are formal and structured while others are informal; some are incremental, some are operational, and some radical or strategic. All such changes together affect one's day-to-day priorities as an individual executive.

Change Agility - the journey is the destination

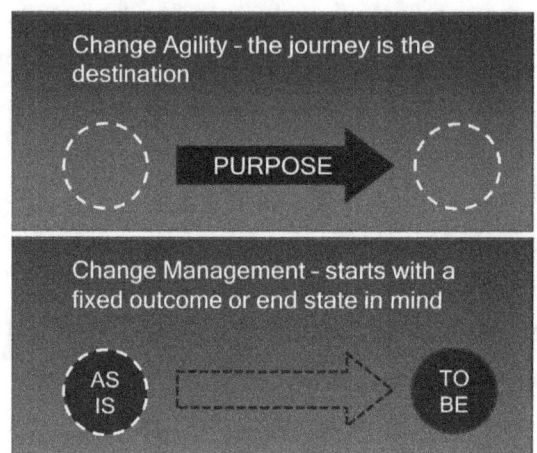

Change Agility - the journey is the destination

PURPOSE

Change Management - starts with a fixed outcome or end state in mind

AS IS

TO BE

People need to accept uncertainty and impermanence

This is only possible if they have mission or purpose which transcends the state they are in and an agile mindset, which is fit for life within complex systems

A purpose which is external to the organization, rather than an internal vision should guide constant adaptation

This lived experience of change as a natural mosaic that reflects the complexity of human systems is our area of interest as organizational psychologists. The diagram above illustrates the different ways that change can be conceptualized. Leaders can start from where people are today and help them move in a controlled way from this relatively stable state toward a conceived end point or outcome. Leaders can try to help people get "there" and attempt to define this end state in precise terms using language internal to the organization, referring to key aspects of the kind of organization they envision it to be in future.

Or, leaders can be change agile. They can assume that in reality, there is no fixed starting point or end point for change, just a journey throughout which we pursue an external purpose or a shared mission in the world that transcends internal organizational boundaries. The implication is that what we experience in an organization is permanent instability. This kind of state of impermanence reflects today's reality for many people in their jobs, their careers, and their organizations.

Here are some features of complex systems that are likely to be relevant to change leadership as corporate life becomes increasingly subject to VUCA forces. Organizations:

- Benefit from disorder (growth occurs because of unpredictability)

- Adapt naturally to changes in the environment through sensing and responding to immediate stimuli

- Explore the environment looking for clues and data that will lead to growth

- Tend to be self-organizing at all levels (i.e., both micro and macro)

- Do not have a fixed blueprint for the future but do move constantly toward overarching mission fulfillment, one step at a time

Change Management practice seeks to reduced disruption due to change.

Change Agility seeks to remove fragility altogether as benefits are always temporary and context is permanently shifting

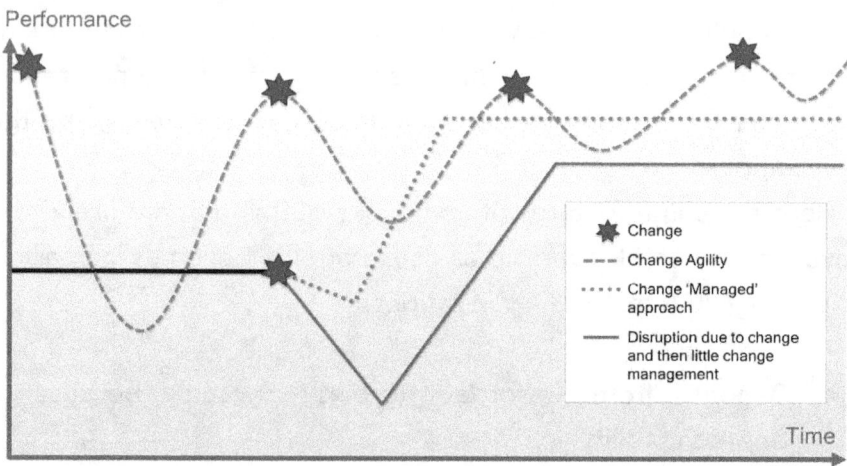

The diagram above illustrates a common view of the human experience of change as a curve. The solid line indicates the view, borne out of early research in the field, that change is naturally disruptive to people and organizations. This is a linear model that is used extensively all over the world to help leaders understand the psychology of change. The key premise of the model is that if change is managed well, people will eventually accept and integrate new ways of working and new ideas into their work.

This "change curve" has been the dominant feature of most change management theory and practice for the last thirty years in organizational psychology. Leaders are shown versions of this curve in almost every program about leading change. Change agility helps individuals, teams, and organizations move away from being prone to disruption due to change. An agile approach to change helps people move toward being able not only to withstand the negative effects of constant change but to turn it into a constant source of benefit. Effectively, they go from being fragile to agile, learning how to harness change through several cycles of change as the diagram illustrates.

The traditional model of change clearly does have relevance to leaders and to organizations. We can recognize aspects of this change curve that do relate to changes we may be experiencing or that we see others experiencing around us. In fact, the change curve (and, indeed, most models of change) emerged from psychological theories of bereavement and grieving in clinical psychology. Change often does feel like a process of grieving for the past—letting go, experimenting with a new way of doing something, then accepting the new reality.

This model is still relevant and helpful for framing how change can be experienced by individuals and at a group level in a whole organization. Participation and involvement helps. Different people could be at different stages in this cycle of change at any point in time. Some will be further ahead, while others may take more time to assimilate changes. Having said this, we have seen individual leaders, teams, and organizations that seem to transcend the emotional roller-coaster ride that many people go on within this kind of bereavement process.

Working on the change capacity in an organization helps leaders to reduce the negative impact of change, both emotionally and in terms of performance. What we find when we are in a highly adaptive, change-capable kind of organization is that people feel less attachment to their roles, their plans, and their current work than to the underlying mission or purpose in the organization. Curiosity, insight, action, and learning are some of the defining features of change in an agile "learning organization" that allow it to integrate new ways of working or adjust to new realities in the external environment. This change-agile model is illustrated below. It draws on a psychological and philosophical appreciation of present, lived experience that we see in certain Asian cultures—a conceptualization that that has also made its way into mainstream psychology in the form of "mindfulness" and various forms of psychotherapy.

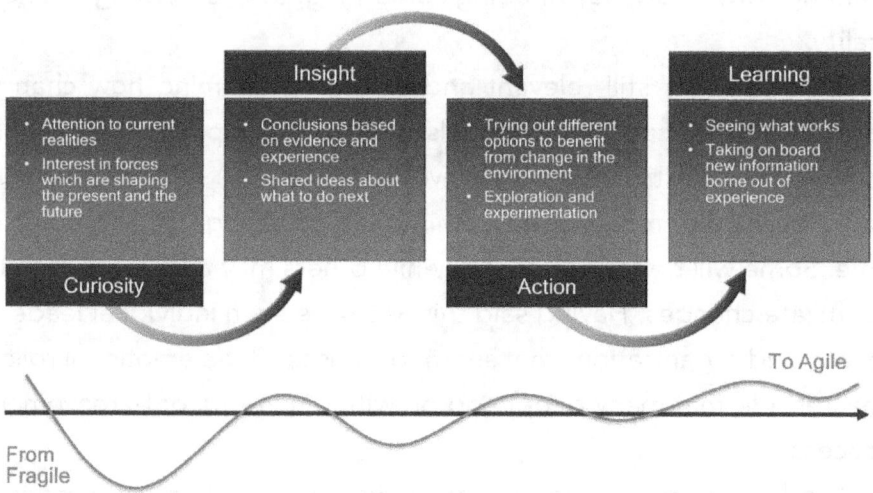

Change Agile practice requires people to treat change as part of their process of learning and simply to see *what works....*

The Change Agile Cycle of Organizational Change is a cycle of learning for the organization and the people in it

Curiosity is the starting point for agile change and for leadership. Curiosity is the basis for transformation—instead of the traditional view of a "burning platform" being necessary for change. The metaphor of the burning platform comes from the idea that people are only willing to take leaps of faith into the future when their current positions are clearly obsolete or being destroyed. Why must we think of change as occurring only when the platform we are on is already burning? Why aren't we always exploring and looking for new platforms for growth and our own transformation?

Leaders surely need to be hungry and be curious. Openness to experience, therefore, plays a big role in change-oriented leadership development. Diverse experiences and exposure are essential to development. A change-agile perspective on the old idea of the burning platform is that organizations need to move from strength to strength and from platform to platform, building new and better platforms constantly as they reach out into the world searching for value. If employees could avoid it, why would they choose to jump from a burning platform into an icy-cold ocean—and why would we ask that of them? This metaphor hardly represents an optimist's view of what change represents. Moving from strength to strength in an agile way is more like navigating across a thickly forested mountain range, constantly seeking unique vantage points to understand and explore new possibilities.

Change agility is about creating frontiers for growth in a crowded and at times unpredictable and risk-laden ecosystem. In this context, the role of strategy is to help leaders make constant choices and to generate a series of short-term advantages within the context of a clear, overarching enterprise purpose.

Continuous learning from diverse experience gained through exploration is at the heart of change agility. Leaders need to engage in active experimentation so that they are learning by doing, not just by studying historic case studies in traditional business school settings. Leaders who demonstrate their practical curiosity, who are interested in what is happening in the world at large, are more likely to create institutions that *benefit* from VUCA rather than become victims of it. Change leadership has historically been all about envisioning a bright or better future and then delivering the changes needed while ensuring the stability of the organization. It is now time to build institutions that are, quite simply, agile by design.

Curiosity with clarity of purpose helps organizations gain from uncertainty. Standard Chartered Bank's brand essence, at the time of this writing, is to be "Here for good." This is positive, in that it does appear to place a social purpose as paramount, and it also suggests reliability. The bank has applied a great deal of strengths-based positive psychology to develop leaders across its global organization to ensure that it is "Here for good" in an uncertain world. Despite some serious challenges with a US regulator relating to alleged money laundering in the Middle East some years ago, the bank has performed solidly.

Leaders at SCB have focused the whole global workforce on the need for a clear sense of responsibility in everything they do, coupled with a change-ready, agile mind-set. The cultural and leadership practices that will assure its longevity and reliability are those that reflect a positive approach to managing uncertainty. Market volatility has seen the downfall or weakening of some formidable financial institutions. Time and reputation will hopefully show that Standard Chartered Bank is indeed "Here for good," and if it is, then this will be at least partly due to its adoption of a purposeful, positive approach to embracing the change needed in the banking sector.

Sound project-management-oriented change practices that include proactive communication, engagement workshops, education, skills training, stakeholder management, and assessment of organizational climate in relation to an individual project or program is covered extensively in existing "how-to" manuals on change. The next generation of change, however, which builds on these basic practices, reflects the need for change agility at the individual and collective level in complex human systems. It will help leaders build learning organizations rather than constantly battle the next wave of change, cajoling staff to "get on board" with "the change" every single time.

The traditional approach is becoming wearisome for leaders and for the people who work in big organizations, where there are likely to be several different changes going on at any one time. It is time for the world to adopt a different paradigm of change and to view it as part of work life. Perhaps for the most agile executives, change is a key personal driver in work and in life.

BITE-SIZED CASE:

Building 'High Performance Culture' in a global services organization

The Scenario: Agile Cultural Transformation

The leadership team of a technology products, services and solutions company in Asia embarked on a program of cultural transformation. This organization might traditionally have commissioned extensive exploratory work first to analyze in depth the current culture, then designed a highly structured, carefully managed change. They might also have hired a large consulting firm and spent millions in fees, working towards a new 'vision' for the company.

In this instance, due to the immediacy of opportunity for growth, the company made bold and immediate changes to certain key levers of performance, such as the way executive-level performance was managed. The whole top cadre of leaders now experiments with new ways of working right away and learns from experience.

An agile approach has yielded insight and learning for the whole organization and generated an instant improvement in business performance. Senior leaders are accelerating change and demonstrating shared ownership for improvement. Learning is happening through less fearful experimentation in response to heightened competition.

What is Change Agility?

Definition:

Change agility at an enterprise level is a mission-critical capability necessary for transformation to occur in a human system that harnesses all the energy in the organization.

We also think change agility is the most critical ability for today's corporate leaders and for teams. It requires people to focus on the right priorities under pressure, use emotion constructively, and take action when and where it counts most to enable change. Change-agile leadership works in the real world, in real time, for results in a VUCA world—where an organization feels less like a machine and more like a natural ecosystem.

Change Agility in is an on-going, informed and holistic response to uncertainty

Agility operates in the rational, emotional, behavioural and spiritual domains of human performance.

Harnessing all of these types of energy simultaneously can improve performance during times of change or uncertainty.

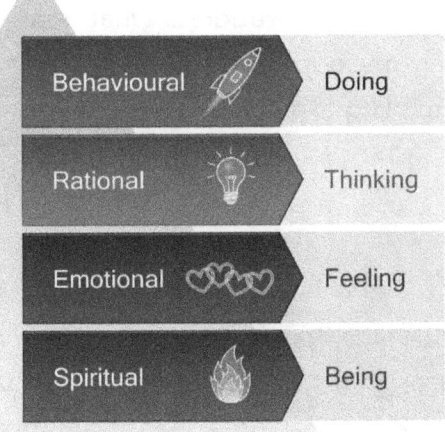

Behavioural	Doing
Rational	Thinking
Emotional	Feeling
Spiritual	Being

The diagram above illustrates the types of energy that are used in times of change or uncertainty, which are related to **how leaders think, how they feel, what they do, and who they are.** These, in turn, can also reflect patterns of thought, emotion, action, and identity across a team or entire organization.

Physical or behavioral agility = Doing

Change is about getting things done in the real world, not just about grappling with complex leadership challenges—or worse, just gazing at the issues rather than seeking to address them. There is no time to gaze at tough issues in a VUCA environment. Behavioral or executional agility requires leaders of change to help mobilize resources and to keep up momentum on critical changes, even when the environment is constantly shifting or appears volatile. They need resilience and courage to keep going while making course corrections to fulfill whatever the mission requires. In military strategy, it is well known that a plan only survives until the first bullet is fired. Similarly, in organizations, planning and coordination are important, but agile execution is what counts toward getting real results. In a sense, good strategy is all about concurrently making choices and enabling execution.

Rational agility = Thinking

There is a great deal of research suggesting that people have different thinking styles that influence how they address problems, deal with change, and manage uncertainty. Agility in the way we think requires us to adopt a "both-and" way of thinking rather than an "either-or" way, for example developing *both* globally consistent *and* locally relevant consumer concepts if we work in a consumer goods company. "Both-and" thinking is about finding ways to manage organizational tensions—to reconcile dilemmas. Many leadership challenges today reflect tensions that need to be reconciled and managed on an ongoing basis rather than problems to be solved. Mental energy that revolves around thinking, decision making and reasoning is critical to leadership in times of change. Leaders have to be able to work with this kind of energy, but not to the detriment of other types of energy required for successful transformational change.

Emotional agility = Feeling

Leaders sometimes overlook feelings, both in themselves and in others. Emotional intelligence research has demonstrated that leaders need to show both self-awareness and social skill to lead change effectively. Agility in the emotional domain requires leaders to go one step further: during times of change and extreme uncertainty, leaders and managers should find ways to manage their feelings and those of others in such a way that they can enable real connections to be made in an organization. People who do not see eye to eye on issues need to be rallied around a common cause, even if their perspectives remain different. An emotionally agile leader is able to help achieve unity in diversity.

Spiritual agility = Being

"Spiritual agility" can be described as working from the position of "knowing who you are and what you stand for." At its heart, the leadership of change today is about relentless pursuit of an organization's core mission or purpose that, at a deeper level, is anchored around a cause or core set of beliefs about what is truly important.

Change agility in the absence of a purpose can feel too impersonal or even clinical. It is a shame that so much leadership education fails to help leaders grasp the importance of values, purpose, and, ultimately, identity. Change management has in the past tended to point people toward a specific end state, target, goal, vision, strategy, or program outcome, such as a cost reduction goal or profitability target. Such outcomes are far from guaranteed in a VUCA world and it is risky to create commitment purely to financial metrics or internally defined outcomes. A collective sense of spirit, a common purpose that transcends targets helps to achieve sustainable outcomes from change. This can be created—with change-agile leadership.

Spiritual energy is harnessed by clarity of purpose with a human cause and a shared strength of identity unifying the team and the organization. This energy is most evident in cause-related organizations and various political movements led by individuals such as Nelson Mandela, or Aung San Suu Kyi. Such individuals demonstrate servant leadership—which is anchored in human purpose and service for the greater good rather than purely personal power, material status, and ambition.

Although we cannot expect corporate leaders at large to behave like social entrepreneurs or philanthropists, we should expect more basic humanity from them at the top level. Many frameworks for change and leadership seem to steer away from this, focusing on the "heart" of change but not its spirit.

The table below shows the progression from change management to change agility. Change-agile leadership enables organizational change that works in the real world, in real time, for accelerated impact.

Change Management	Change Agility
Leader driven: top-down	Distributed: top-down and bottom up
Visionary and transformational leaders who determine a future that others need to understand and embrace	Purposeful and collective leadership with a range of possible and potential futures informed by a diverse organization
Overcoming resistance to change to status quo	Removing any sense of a status quo
Stakeholder engaged	Stakeholder driven and owned
Realizes benefits after implementation	Realizes benefits from day one
Project managed and phased	Rapidly prototyped, tested, and iterated
Team of change agents drive "the change'	Temporary, self-forming teams enable experiments
Need to think yourself into new ways of acting	Act yourself into new ways of thinking

Change management helps to implement a particular strategy by successfully "taking people with you" as you navigate an inevitable period of instability. The core assumption about change in this approach is that it requires leaders who own the vision for the organization's "end state." Other core assumptions are that people naturally fear the change and that it impacts performance negatively unless it is "managed." This paradigm can be helpful at an early stage of change maturity. But change agility requires leaders to make change feel like part of work and like a largely positive experience that unlocks creativity while also being sensitive to the fact that certain types of change can have painful impact in the short term.

BITE-SIZED CASE:
Chief Learning Officer in Asia

The Scenario: Need for a High-Performance Culture and Stronger Leadership Capability for Long-Term Sustainability of Bank Performance

A newly appointed chief learning officer for a large Asian financial institution found that the internal culture and leadership capablity needed to change to meet the growth and performance expectations of the owners and investors. The CEO and board also confirmed this in initial discussions.

The CLO undertook a review that showed a particular need for change leadership skills at all levels. The bank was slow to react to market movements and to implement change, which affected its competitiveness. The CLO created a holistic program of leadership development, in consultation with the board, for every layer of leadership and management so they could understand how to improve their approach to change. This was done with direct input and involvement from the CEO. The CLO himself took risks and showed real courage as the new "leadership academy" unsettled some of the old guard.

The bank has stayed the course and is already seeing improvements in measures such as employee engagement because leadership is becoming more agile.

In a VUCA world, some projects or individual programs of change can be managed well with traditional change management methods. In general, what we observe is that the desire for stability means that progress toward a vision or some kind of "end state" at an overall enterprise level can be frustrating. When executives are asked about their actual change challenges, it is evident how complex, relentless, and full of permanent dilemmas their world really is. Managing such complexity requires clarity of mission, the ability to reframe events mentally and emotionally, and making things happen in anticipation of events rather than in response to them.

Change agility is a capability and facet of both leadership and organizational culture rather than purely a management method. Through this capability, organizations can turn permanent instability into a source of value, a competitive advantage in pursuit of external purpose rather than internal excellence. The world we are in requires leaders to find opportunity in uncertainty and not to shy away from the unknown. Change-agile leaders build change capability within an organization to drive performance. People within such organizations are liberated and empowered to reconcile their everyday dilemmas creatively. Change agility requires executives to go deep into questions about shared mission and to be permanently aware of their shifting context. The people who work with such leaders are more ready for change and also eager to harness its power.

We find there are myriad examples of how leading in a VUCA world requires change agility. In the mobile devices sector, in high-risk industries like the energy sector, and in creative technology firms, a culture of innovation and the ability to respond to VUCA forces all reflect the quality of leadership and culture in the organization.

CHANGE CHALLENGES

More Industry Examples

The Mobile Devices Sector: From good to great—and then to obscurity? The mobile devices industry is one of the least predictable and most competitive sectors around. The extent of competition is palpable if you walk into any mobile handset store in the world. Only a few years ago at the time of this writing, Nokia was king—seemingly unstoppable with its range of mobile phones and smartphones. Research In Motion, the maker of Blackberry, had a strong position as the leading manufacturer of business devices. Motorola was also a strong player, with the occasional hit product. What is amazing is how quickly huge changes in consumer tastes and the competitive landscape have affected these companies.

In Nokia's and Motorola's cases, this is especially interesting, as these were exemplar organizations that had reinvented themselves more than once. For Nokia, reinvention seemed to be in the corporate DNA. Once superbly innovative global manufacturers that were known for quality and innovation, they have slipped into decline. Nokia's and Motorola's new parent companies may help to reinvigorate their mobile device businesses. The ability to demonstrate leadership and organizational agility—to read the competitive environment, to build aspiration in a global workforce, to get aligned internally and then accelerate the deployment of winning solutions constantly—seems to have been strong at some point in these firms, and then it eroded. In any technology-based industry that is dynamic and has attributes of VUCA, a capacity for change is the key to sustained advantage, though it is hard to develop and easily lost.

Safety and Risk Management Reflects Executive and Enterprise Agility

The *Deepwater Horizon* oil spill in 2010 is a notorious example of a huge industrial accident in a global energy company: British Petroleum. Companies like BP and their leaders are constantly under intense public scrutiny. BP's subsequent and ongoing safety efforts require cultural agility and adaptability. Fukushima Daiichi nuclear power plant, operated by Tokyo Electric Power Company, experienced a catastrophic operational meltdown in 2011 after the terrible earthquake and tsunami in Japan.

One of the most researched and well-known safety-related tragedies in modern history is the space shuttle *Challenger* disaster of 1986, when the vessel broke apart seventy-three seconds into its flight, leading to the deaths of its seven crew members. This was found to be due to certain cultural weaknesses at NASA.

The Bhopal disaster, also referred to as the "Bhopal gas tragedy," was a gas leak incident in India that is considered the world's worst industrial disaster. It occurred in 1984 at the Union Carbide India Limited (UCIL) pesticide plant in Bhopal.

In all of these cases and several others, weaknesses in organizational culture have led to tragic, unintended consequences. Implementing safety in high-risk industries is not just about training or safety procedures. The mental, emotional, and physical energies—and the purpose of all leaders—should reflect a duty of care toward staff, society, and the environment. The ability to anticipate, prioritize, handle, and mitigate unpredictable issues in a large organization reflects its change agility.

How Google is Unlocking People's Spiritual Energy: Search Inside Yourself

What if people can use contemplative practices to help them succeed in life and at work? In other words, what if contemplative practices can be made beneficial both to people's careers and to business bottom lines?

–Chade-Meng Tan, Google

Google has been using mindfulness training in the form of its now-famous Search Inside Yourself program for employees since 2007. The program combines various aspects of psychology and meditation to help Google find the deeper inner resources to exercise greater "self-mastery"—the ability to be a master of one's thoughts, emotions, and behavior.

Google is a global exemplar in unlocking the mental, emotional, physical, and spiritual energies of people who work at the company—for business benefit. They hire bright and motivated people, clearly. However, every single aspect of their culture, from the design of their buildings to the language they use and the content of programs such as Search Inside Yourself, is aligned with their purpose as an organization. So, their focus is not just on bringing in people who demonstrate the right qualities. The company creates an environment, in a holistic sense, that then reinforces the kind of culture that helps Google be a world leader.

Google is an employer of choice globally because it sets out to live the company's values and also helps people build career identity. These are all elements of change agility at work.

BITE-SIZED CASE:

CIO of a Middle Eastern Conglomerate

The Scenario: Shared Services Implementation for a Family-Owned Business with Several Business Units and Operations in Eleven Countries

The chief information officer of a large private company headquartered in the Middle East completed a detailed study into the effectiveness of its IT support organizations and systems. He found that a complete transformation of the IT capability was needed; it took three years and a multimillion-dollar investment.

Prior to his arrival, his own leadership team historically had had a very poor track record in implementing technology change. He took the time to include development of their own personal change leadership skills. He also commissioned his program office to build an agile methodology for change management and for executing the transformation that was deployed across the business.

The approach addressed every aspect of the transformation needed: technical, process, and people aspects. When it came to the human side of the change, his team constantly engaged key stakeholders openly and honestly about how it would affect them. He delivered a transformation that affected thousands of IT system users as well as 250 IT staff members. He was careful to align the program with the company's mission and strategy, securing strong sponsorship from the owner and board from the outset. He had to change course several times but did not lose his nerve at any point, demonstrating his own agility.

BITE-SIZED CASE:

Head of Risk

The Scenario: Transformation of Risk Management for a Large Asian Investment Company

The chief risk officer for an investment company arrived at her new institution after a successful career in risk consulting. She had been transferred from the United States to Singapore for her new role. She found that the culture and leadership style in the organization was fundamentally different from the style of leadership she was used to. After a year in the post, it was clear to her that risk management needed a fundamental change in every aspect—of the organization, structure, rewards, training, careers, and, most important, the ways of working that supported risk management.

The evidence she had showed that enormous gaps existed. She commissioned a study externally that gave even more weight to her push to implement several changes. These changes threatened the status quo in the organization in terms of how investment decisions were made. As she initiated the changes she felt were needed, with some consultation and engagement with her peers and subordinates and with strong board backing, she experienced resistance. Her peers felt she was an obstacle to business growth.

Her reaction was to fight this resistance head on, as the case for change was so clear. Unfortunately, her support at senior levels waned. She encountered significant political pressure to ease off, and the change she envisioned faltered. She realized that she needed to pay much more attention to the need for alignment of key influencers and needed to demonstrate the link that risk management had to the company's core mission.

THREE KEY IDEAS TO TAKE AWAY FROM THIS SECTION

1 *Volatility*, *uncertainty*, *complexity*, and *ambiguity* are dominant aspects of today's business environment. In very important ways, they affect the way you need to lead and manage change. Change in organizations is complex and unpredictable.

2 Change agility is not just about helping people get from point A to point B. In a VUCA world, it is also about being change agile yourself, building an agile team, and developing an agile organization—so you are always ready to change.

3 Change agility is a mind-set and a set of behaviors that operate at all levels and harness your mental, emotional, physical, and innermost spiritual energy to help you navigate change. In a VUCA world, you need to have strength of purpose, empathy with others, and courage to take action.

Will it make the boat go faster?

—Ben Hunt-Davis, Olympic
gold-medal rower

SECTION 2

CHANGE AGILITY IN ACTION

Having shared our perspective on the challenge of change in today's business environment and how this challenge is becoming increasing complex, we will now discuss the change agility model in more depth. We'll explore how change agility helps you get results, what the main success factors are, and how these success factors can be applied to different leadership challenges.

We'll explore leadership dilemmas and how executives tend to respond to them: these represent important and typical day-to-day tensions of corporate leaders. What we find is that executives naturally show preferences for different kinds of change. They can also show psychological preferences for ways to deal with complex problems. We will share the main "leadership archetypes" and how they relate to dilemmas you might typically face.

We will also provide a perspective on how the process of transformation requires an approach to leadership that uses change agility practices, turning "change resistance" as far as possible into a source of positive energy in the organization.

Change Agility Gets Results

There is considerable evidence that leadership and culture really do matter when it comes to getting results. Both are key drivers of a company's long-term financial performance and adaptability. In particular, a robust finding in research on organizational culture and performance is that companies that strengthen their ability to adapt, by applying specific leadership and cultural practices, substantially outperform those that don't.

In one survey of ninety-four large companies, executives were asked to report on their organizations' various change leadership practices and the degree of adaptability in their cultures. In this study, ten years of these companies' financial performance was reviewed. Several aspects of change agility were found to have strong links to superior growth in net income and stock value. Research by various global consulting organizations has shown that successful organizations and leaders show change agility.

In general, change agility can be described broadly as the ability to change and respond well to external market dynamics, if not anticipate or even shape market movements. In an era of market volatility in several sectors and radical, rapid changes often underpinned by technological change, the attention being given to this area of leadership capability is not surprising. It is a critical area of organizational performance. We have set out to broaden and deepen both the definition and application of change agility.

Our own strong conclusion as business psychologists is that powerful evidence shows that building the capacity for change in organizations—and the use of sound change management methods within individual initiatives—is not only worthwhile, it can be a source of competitive advantage. The framework we share is designed to improve the return on investment from change, supporting strategy execution and business transformation. In the following sections, we hope to show you how you can harness change in relentless pursuit of purpose.

Change-Agile Leadership Harnesses Change

Building on the definition we shared in the previous section of this guide, here we describe the critical capabilities of leaders, teams, and whole organizations that compose change agility. The four types of energy, rational, emotional, behavioral, and spiritual, can be mapped onto success factors of change agility: *aspiration*, *alignment and acceleration*, and the need for *common purpose*.

This is a holistic (rather than a partial) model for developing agile organizations. We find that models for change often emphasize only certain elements; few attempt to draw together all of the different kinds of energy needed to be agile. In particular, existing models have focused, quite rightly, on bringing emotional aspects of change and organizational culture into the picture. This has been a positive development. However, few models seem to anchor the whole process of transformation in organizational purpose explicitly enough. Far too much change practice is anchored instead only in targets or results rather than in shared human purpose. Change that is driven by shared purpose tends to be self-sustaining—even leaderless, but with an abundance of leadership.

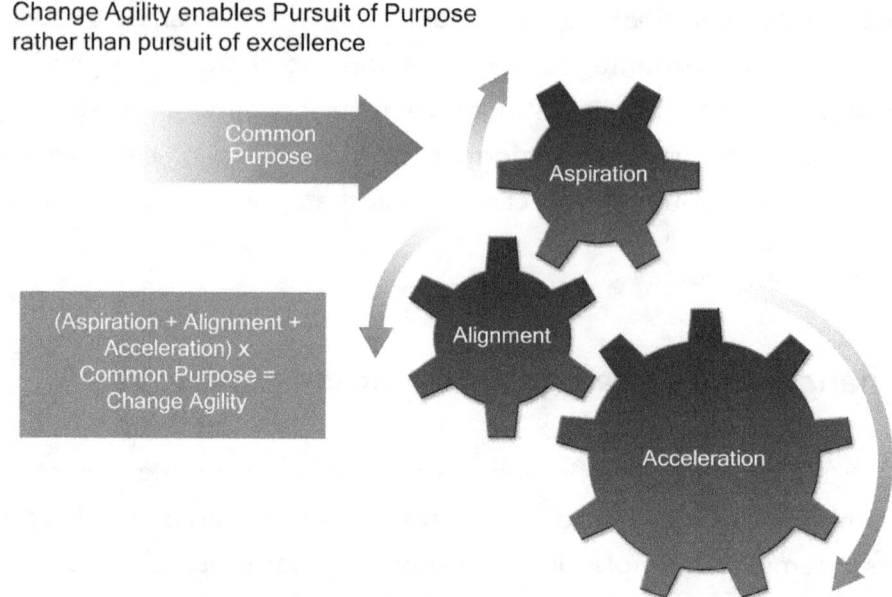

Change Agility enables Pursuit of Purpose
rather than pursuit of excellence

Aspiration and alignment together draw most heavily on rational energy and emotional energy, while *acceleration* draws most on
behavioral (or physical) energy. Spiritual energy underpins the creation of common purpose, which reflects an organization's identity:
the cause that people within the organization feel they represent.

Increasingly, we see that in new generations entering the workforce around the world, a sense of meaning and purpose is absolutely
critical to their engagement and identification with their employer.
Organizations that struggle to articulate the "why" of strategy and
change in a compelling way will find it increasingly challenging to
engage younger generations in their strategic agendas. Younger generations may not be fired up by a desire to, say, "double revenues in
five years," or "be great" or "number one," or "delight our customers
by being a customer-centric organization." These are good outcomes
that most people understand and in some way relate to. In fact, without

clarity of desired outcomes, strategic transformation efforts can falter. However, even with stock options, bonuses, or personal equity ownership stakes that are connected to overall corporate outcomes, it is unlikely that for many employees and managers, these sorts of corporate ambition statements constitute anything close to a purpose.

Change Agility Success Factors all work together in harmony and constitute a model for whole leadership, not partial leadership

Aspiration	Alignment	Acceleration	Unintended Outcomes For Leaders and Organizations
✓	✓		May not have sufficient delivery and execution capacity to make things happen, despite clarity of shared purpose. There may not be enough energy to keep going despite setbacks and changes in direction. There may be burnout and lethargy due to change
✓		✓	May be derailed by resistance, internal conflicts and hidden agendas even if people understand the direction of travel and are attempting to make changes. Internal silos may be competing with each other rather than collaboration. Personal needs may take over
	✓	✓	May have emotional and practical momentum for change but may not have ensured that people are moving in the same direction. There may not be sufficient clarity, shared meaning and sense of real stretch to create sustained capacity for change in a team or business. As a leader, without sufficient aspiration, there will be little to anchor change in over the long term

The table above illustrates the idea that the key success factors of change agility are interdependent and mutually reinforcing. Aspiration promotes collective clarity of purpose. Alignment engenders trust. Acceleration enables execution. These three success factors are each composed of further subcomponents. Each of the factors of change agility can be developed for performance improvements, particularly during transformational change.

Every area is critical for reaping the full benefit of change agility. It is an integrated model. If one of the factors is missing in a leader, a team, or an organizational unit, over the long term, there may be unintended consequences when trying to deal with uncertainty or in the execution of strategy. Although at certain times (for instance, during a crisis) creating acceleration may be more important than creating aspiration, it is clear that in the long run, for an organization to build strong change capability (particularly when the landscape is uncertain), aspiration, alignment, and acceleration are all key success factors of performance. Common purpose acts as the central focal point for all action.

The reality for most of us is that we do not have natural strengths in every single aspect of change agility. It is to be expected that its requirements come naturally to different people. The key to successful leadership during uncertain times is that leaders work together to apply their different strengths and capabilities. In a team, ideally there is a balance of all of the different success factors of change agility and an appreciation of the contribution each of them can make to complex organizational problems.

Although change in a VUCA world is likely to be fluid, clearly there are also frequently phases that a team or business goes through in implementing change. In the early phases of large initiatives with defined objectives, it may well be that time spent to create clear and compelling aspirations for the initiative, linked to the overarching purpose of the organization, is critical. As the aspirations become clear, increasing levels of team and organizational alignment need to be visible. Emotional connection with the initiative is necessary to generate sustained action. Once there is sufficient critical mass of aspiration and alignment in a team or a business, then the ability to drive sustained acceleration into a shared future becomes not only possible, but a natural progression.

Change Agility Success Factors

Each area of capability can be
measured with 3 sub components:

Aspiration

- Purposeful
- Integrative
- Inclusive

Alignment

- Constructive
- Creative
- Versatile

Acceleration:

- Responsive
- Adaptive
- Resilient

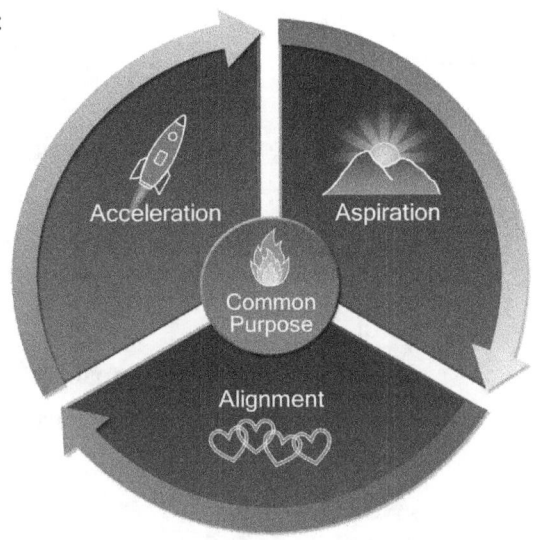

The diagram above outlines the success factors that constitute change agility.

We've found that organizations can have biases toward different areas of the model. In some companies we may find a natural bias for edge and for action, but in the absence of alignment or an appropriate sense of collective aspiration and direction, this can create confusion or even genuine chaos. Alternatively, an organization can be very strong at internal dialogue needed to generate consensus but less well equipped to accelerate progress because of poor risk appetite or low levels of resilience in the face of operational pressures. One of the aims of development is to achieve greater balance across all of the different capabilities, using all the energies.

Description of the success factors of change agility

Aspiration

This success factor is about building collective clarity of mission to harness change and turn uncertainty into opportunity by being:

Purposeful
- Works with deep sense of purpose, creating clear short- and long-term goals and with intrinsic motivation, even without a clear "blueprint" or end state to work toward

Integrative
- Integrates polarized perspectives to reconcile dilemmas in pursuit of purpose, overcoming personal or cultural biases and helping others to do the same

Inclusive
- Creates collective clarity of mission and common identity, building a sense of unity across internal silos and cultures, transcending politics. Builds the organization's capability during tough times rather than allow crisis to pull people apart

Alignment

This success factor is about seeking leverage from diversity, removing internal silos, and building readiness for any kind of change by being:

Constructive
- Creates deep connections with others and between others to harness diversity, creating creative conflict rather than resistance. Provides both support and challenge

Creative
- Is comfortable with problem solving, handling seemingly conflicting data from multiple sources to respond well to external trends. Relies on both personal intuition and rigorous analysis to form deep insight and to influence others

Versatile
- Works through networks rather than traditional structures, constantly reinforcing the need for organizational agility. Also puts in place streamlined controls, high-quality risk management, and robust decision making processes

Acceleration

This success factor is about building momentum and generating a sustained response to collective enterprise challenges, combining speed and control to get results.

Responsive
- Works with pace across boundaries, while mitigating risks, to lead change. Uses both formal processes and informal methods to take action and achieve goals, taking into account mission-critical data

Adaptive
- Shifts personal style, communication, behavior, and mind-set to accommodate new information or needs of the organization

Resilient
- Has the emotional capacity to learn from failure and to have courage when challenged. Responds to high levels of sustained pressure in a way that creates opportunity out of crisis

The most powerful way to think about these success factors is to remember that they apply to individual leaders, to teams, and to whole departments or organizations. They scale up into team and organizational capabilities quite readily. A team, for example, can exhibit significant versatility and resilience but limited sense of purpose or creativity. Similarly, an organization can be purposeful and inclusive without the equally important responsiveness and action orientation.

Clearly, in an organization with most leaders demonstrating the success factors to a high level and in equal measure, we should also notice that the climate of the leadership group and the culture in general reflects this balanced and whole leadership capability. A well-balanced and complete leadership team should demonstrate a high level of overall change agility in its behavior. Balance is an important aim for development of change readiness.

Change Agility Helps Reconcile Cultural Dilemmas

Extensive psychological research on "cognitive style" has shown that executives can have personal preferences that may act as sources of unconscious bias in the way they solve problems or deal with change and complexity. On one hand, some executives prefer to deal with change in a gradual, incremental way, step by step, building on the work that has already been done. This approach works well in a reasonably stable operational environment where incremental improvements are needed. On the other hand, others prefer more radical change and "outside-the-box" solutions to challenges. They might seek to drive highly innovative strategies to create value for the enterprise.

These two styles are traditionally seen as opposites, with the more cautious, methodical style essentially showing a "tight" leadership style and the other a "looser" approach, to put it simplistically. In fact, we also find that organizations demonstrate these tight and loose features in the way that internal cultural dilemmas are handled. Some organizations are culturally better at gradual process improvements and a carefully project-managed approach to change, while others may be more inclined toward radical, blue-sky thinking and the naturally chaotic form of change that can sometimes go with it.

Cultural dilemmas are part and parcel of the challenge of change in any big organization. We have identified seven of the most common dilemmas in organizations and shown that for each one, approaches generally reflect either a "tight," more conservative way of thinking or a "loose," progressive way.

The important thing about "loose" and "tight" styles is that both have their merits, and which is preferable depends entirely on context, so there is no prescription to follow here. Actually, much research into leadership and organization strategy has shown that the key to managing complexity is to be able to *combine* loose and tight ways of thinking about dilemmas. Our experience tells us that much of the complexity leaders experience is related in some way to one or several of these dilemmas—and that these dilemmas reflect *cultural orientations* in the organization.

The seven particularly common dilemmas we come across relate to seven common areas of cultural tension in large organizations: change, planning, risk, products and services, work environment, decision making, and priority setting. These are critical aspects of organization culture that leadership can impact and often must navigate during any business transformation or program execution process. These areas reflect domains of work in which leaders can shape culture and need to make both personal and collective choices.

Cultural orientation is relevant to almost any kind of transformation, expansion, cost reduction, structural change, systems change, product-related changes, and so on. So, in a way, tight/loose orientation transcends specific context and is always present as an influencer of strategy and behavior. The table below illustrates that change agility requires the *integration* of loose and tight cultural orientations. Enterprise leadership challenges can be broken down into cultural dilemmas that leaders need to reconcile constantly.

Seven Dilemmas Inherent to Different Cultural Orientations

Tight Organization ⟷	Loose Organization
Adaptive change	Radical change
Short-term planning	Long-term planning
Low risk, low return	High risk, high return
Standardized products/services	Customized products/services
Structured working	Flexible working
Hierarchical decisions	Entrepreneurial decisions
Profit-driven business	Values-driven business

The areas of organizational culture—the cultural orientations—from which these seven cultural dilemmas arise are:

Change orientation. Should we build on existing practices for generating improvements and ensuring we are delivering results today? Or do something radical? Being more radical requires us to rethink our business models to transform performance. The answer is that in today's world, most senior executives are tasked with doing both—delivering improvement every day and radical step changes in the medium-to-longer term.

Planning orientation. Should we focus on this quarter's number or the three-to-five-year strategy? The answer is that most executives we work with need to deliver aggressive quarterly (or annual) targets while also showing they have a long-term plan in place to grow the business, usually exponentially.

Risk orientation. Should we minimize risk or maximize returns? Again, what many executives learn is that their role isn't either to generate exceptional growth or just manage risks well, but to keep a very firm eye on risk while delivering exceptional financial returns to shareholders. Investors want well-managed growth and value creation from corporate executives, not risk-free stagnation in the value of their assets.

Product development and services orientation. Should we have standardized, global products and services or customize them locally? It seems clear in the area of product or service design, development, and marketing that in most multinational business today, no matter what sector, the challenge is not to make trade-offs between global, regional, and locally driven design but how to create harmony between them. Products, services, and brands need to have global scale and relevance while also being attractive to local customers, clients, and consumers (this set of qualities is also known as "glocal").

Working orientation. Should we use structured working practices and operational metrics to track people's performance or allow people the freedom to decide what works best for them? In most organizations, parts of the business can be metric driven and reliant on robust processes (for example, customer service, IT support, and supply chain). They need highly structured ways of working. Other parts of the organization may need for much more flexible roles and working practices (for example, an internal consulting group that does project management across functions).

However, in any part of an organization, we find the need for people to have both sufficient structure to do their jobs well and sufficient freedom to create their own solutions to problems (or choose how they work to maximize their own productivity). This can be true of customer service as much as of any other part of the business. Again, leaders need to resolve the tension between such considerations, bringing together structured practices and sufficient autonomy for people to exercise their own judgment. This blend of approaches might relate to working hours and patterns as well as ways of working. People in a customer-facing team might have fixed hours and working patterns at certain times and more flexible options to work on improvement projects or engage in personal development at other times, for example.

Decision making orientation. Should we make decisions through a hierarchical process or give people room to make mistakes and experiment? Decision making is traditionally done within carefully defined parameters: decision rights. Decisions rights are held within different management layers ascribed different levels of authority around expenditure or investments, for example.

While this is fine in principle, in a VUCA world, people at the front line of an organization increasingly need to be able to make (and receive) decisions virtually instantly. Leaders need to create a climate with a degree of control plus the possibility of front line empowerment. In an empowered organization, layers are kept to a minimum; the layers that do exist have a clear, value-added role to play in decision making that is supported by reliable data gained from the front line. Change agility is the antidote in this case to what many employees and managers experience as "pointless bureaucracy." However, we don't believe that all hierarchy is defunct—just that if it exists, it needs to have demonstrable value to the people who work in the organization.

Priority setting orientation. Should our priorities be driven by the bottom line or by our corporate values and public reputation? This is an important and deep tension today, especially given several recent examples of companies focusing entirely on profits instead of living up to their own values and stated codes of conduct. The financial sector in general is a great case in point, especially in the during the US mortgage bubble that led to well-known and terrible human consequences.

It has become a truism that companies need to live their values even as they generate profits. Business reality is that this may be difficult to achieve sometimes, and leaders may often feel they need to compromise one goal, the other, or both. Growing a business in certain markets may require organizations to make some quite fundamental choices given the political, social or ethical practices in some of these markets can be at odds with their espoused values. Change-agile leaders will find ways to build great global businesses while staying true to the values of their organizations. Both countries and corporations need to find ways to grow responsibly—an idea that is at the heart of change agility.

Seven Cultural Orientations which give rise
to cultural dilemmas

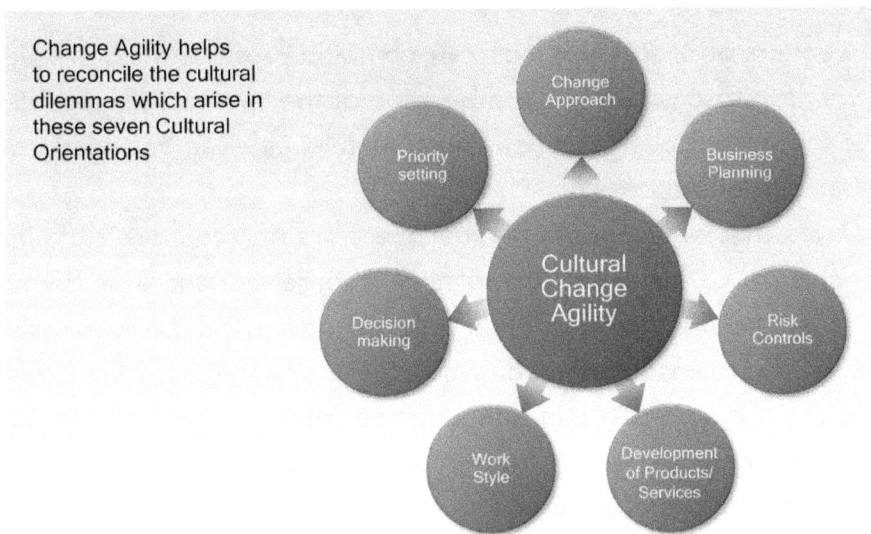

Change Agility helps
to reconcile the cultural
dilemmas which arise in
these seven Cultural
Orientations

The diagram above illustrates the seven critical aspects of both leadership and organizational culture. Any attempt to build change agility must manage the natural tension that occurs in each of these seven areas. The ability to reconcile leadership dilemmas rather than just solve problems is the essence of leadership in a VUCA world. We regularly find that clients become tangled in lengthy debates about issues that reflect these dilemmas. Much research and experience says that the mind-set needed in a globalized, complex business environment requires "both-and" thinking, not "either-or" thinking. This means being able to optimize and apply *both loose and tight* ways of leading.

Change Leader Archetypes

Leaders and organizations can combine loose and tight styles, as we have discussed. The combination of the two actually results in four change agility archetypes for leadership: *catalyst, balancer, strategizer,* and *operator.*

Note that we do not imply that there are only four ways of leading change or managing complexity in organizations—far from it. However, from a developmental point of view, it can help individual leaders and teams to reflect on which archetype they most emulate in their own behavior. This, in turn, enables them to inquire further into the thinking patterns, behavioral patterns, and emotions that may underpin their preferences.

We directly derived the archetypes from the ways executives prefer to operate in relation to each of the seven cultural orientations we outlined above. The important thing for you as a leader to reflect on is the extent to which you balance or combine the tight and loose approaches to each dilemma. If you tend to sit in the middle on each, then you probably prefer balance. If you integrate opposites—which is very hard—then you prefer to reconcile dilemmas. If you tend to prefer the tight end of each dilemma, you may have a rigorous, operational focus. If you prefer the loose end of each dilemma, then you may be more of a blue-sky thinker and are naturally strategic in your style.

The mistake we believe many leadership modelers make is to propose that leadership at the enterprise level needs to be predominantly "strategic." In reality, at all levels, people must demonstrate both certain operational and strategic capabilities to manage change well.

Change Agility Combines 'Loose' and 'Tight' Leadership

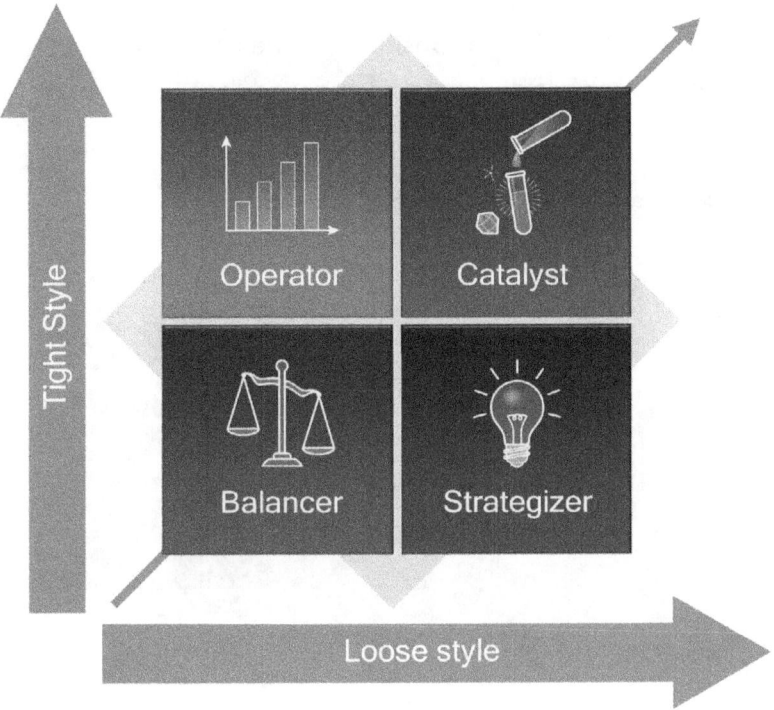

The archetypes reflect the routines or preferences of individuals, teams, and whole organizations.

- *Balancer.* Tries to balance loose and tight styles but finds it hard to combine them. Can be indecisive and slow to act at times.

- *Operator.* Handles change and VUCA with an incremental and controlled approach. Can be too tactical to the detriment of longer term or bigger picture thinking at times.

- *Strategizer.* Handles change with "innovation." Can lack pragmatism and be strategic to the detriment of operational realities.

- *Catalyst.* Combines opposite styles flexibly and thrives in VUCA. Handles complexity well and can lead "at the edge of chaos."

Change Agility Combines Different, Even Opposing Perspectives on an Issue to Create Synergy – Agile Organizations can Synergize...

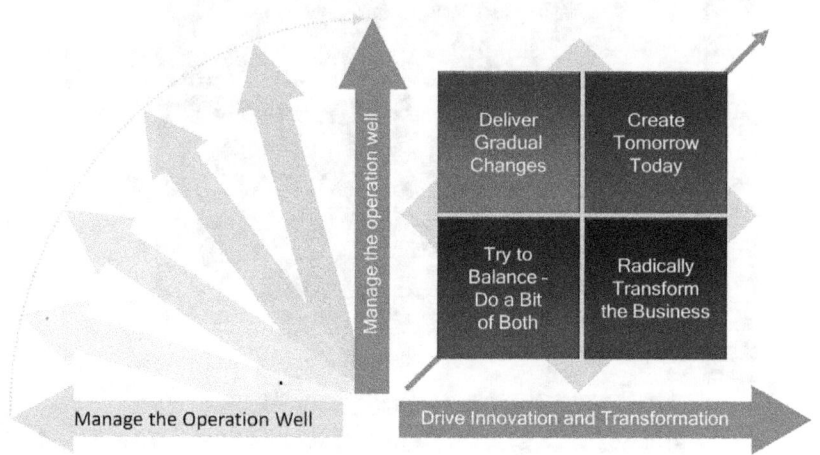

As the diagram above shows, the loose and tight styles of leadership can be combined in different ways. A leader, team, or indeed organization can demonstrate any of these combinations. The ideal position is an integrated approach, combining both loose and tight ways of leading change or managing complex issues related to organizational dilemmas. The ability to do both—to be operationally strong and strategically oriented—is important to successful change.

In fact, the diagram represents loose and tight ways of thinking and behaving as not opposites at all. We represent the styles as simply two dimensions of culture and leadership that, when combined, tend to get the best long-term results.

BITE-SIZED CASE:

Role of the Corporate Center

The Scenario: Corporate Center Design
That Combines Loose and Tight

Several growing multinational organizations and public services struggle with the designs of their corporate headquarters or corporate centers. They must support the rest of their businesses efficiently and effectively.

Our experience is that the key design principle for an effective corporate center is to combine loose and tight approaches to supporting the rest of the organization. In some areas of policy and strategy, the approach needs to be loose (for example, in local go-to-market strategies) and in others tight (for example, in establishing brand standards).

A corporate structure has to be both loose and tight to support profitable growth. In global organizations that successfully internationalize (like Starbucks or Yum! Brands), a strong corporate center supports global operations and franchises. Equally, the regional and local teams are properly mandated to drive growth in emerging markets like India.

The Change Agility Leadership Archetypes

The Catalyst

Change Agility Combines 'Loose' and 'Tight' Leadership. Catalysts combine seemingly opposed leadership styles – they show most versatility.

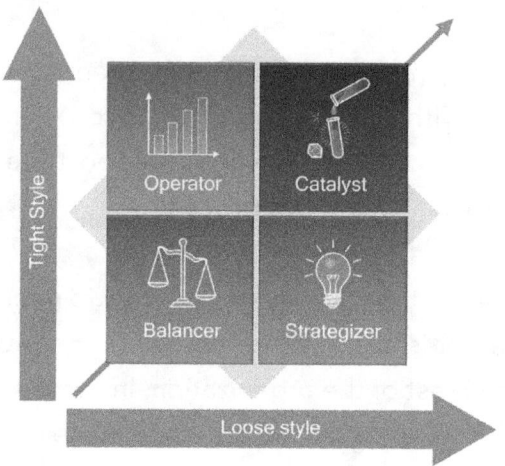

A *catalyst* is likely to be someone who thrives in a volatile, uncertain, complex, and ambiguous environment. Catalysts feel able to integrate ways of working that are fundamentally different—to combine "loose" and "tight" leadership styles during times of change. Catalysts are likely to exhibit agile ways of thinking, feeling, doing, and being, which can help make change happen more successfully. The catalyst archetype demonstrates and embodies change agility.

It is extremely difficult for leaders, teams, or organizations to demonstrate every success factor consistently to the maximum extent. It serves to highlight a combination of behaviors that are likely to help you win in a VUCA world. Many features of a related concept, "emotional intelligence," are also present in the catalyst style. Emotional intelligence uses awareness, regulation, and application of emotional signals to lead and guide change.

If you think this is the archetype you most likely resemble, you are likely to thrive in high-pressure, changeable, and volatile environments. You are likely to handle complexity well and can handle leading at the edge of chaos. You probably prefer to create common purpose; you build aspiration, alignment, and acceleration into your own leadership practice and into how others work. You may prefer to integrate loose and tight ways of managing change, making decisions, and operating as a manager or leader. This potentially shows up as a highly versatile and adaptive style, showing an ability to focus on the big picture while pursuing immediate gains at the same time. You are likely to show some hallmarks of self-mastery and change mastery.

Even if you feel this is your preferred archetype, though, you might not always exhibit the relevant behaviors consistently. This kind of mismatch between your preferences and your actual behavior can occur with any aspect of your personality and is influenced by circumstance. There is always room to grow your ability to live the change agility success factors, and it is worth looking for ways to improve, even if you feel you are already "there."

The Balancer

A balancer usually prefers to balance the operational and strategic elements of leadership in times of change with no strong desire to work in one way or the other. In essence, a balancer attempts to do both at different times but finds this usually involves a great deal of compromise. This way of working is very different from reconciling dilemmas by genuinely integrating what feel like opposite styles. For example the difference between achieving "work-life balance" and achieving "work-life integration" is subtle but important. To a catalyst, the difference is intuitive and natural. Integration involves sucking the juice out of all areas of life, including work, not just compromising.

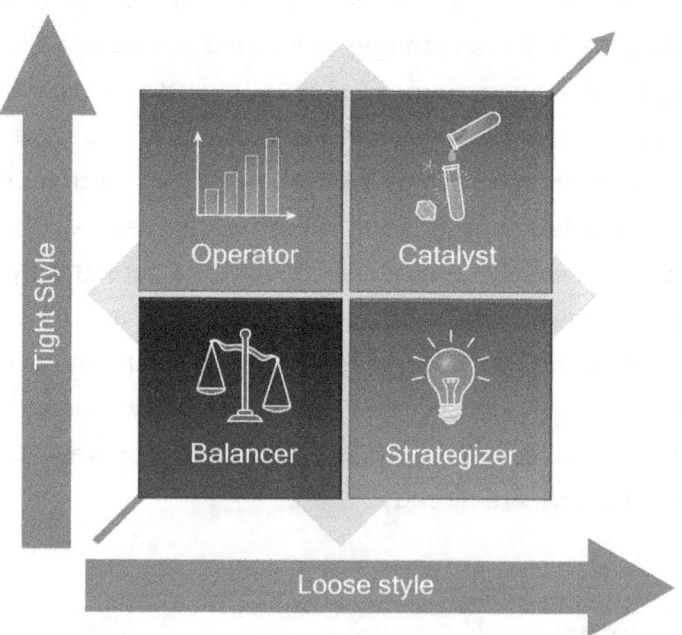

Balancers try to balance different orientations but do not combine opposites

If you feel the balancer may be your closest archetype, you may feel pulled in two different directions at times—on one hand toward a focus on the practical aspects of change or on operational realities and on the other, toward a need to create clarity around the bigger picture or end state. It is possible to be hijacked by change or uncertainty because in your attempt to balance different considerations, you may appear indecisive or confused under pressure. In fact, you may oscillate between periods of being very operationally focused and periods of working on more strategic goals. You might feel torn between the two, and this may manifest itself behaviorally as "sitting on the fence."

The Operator

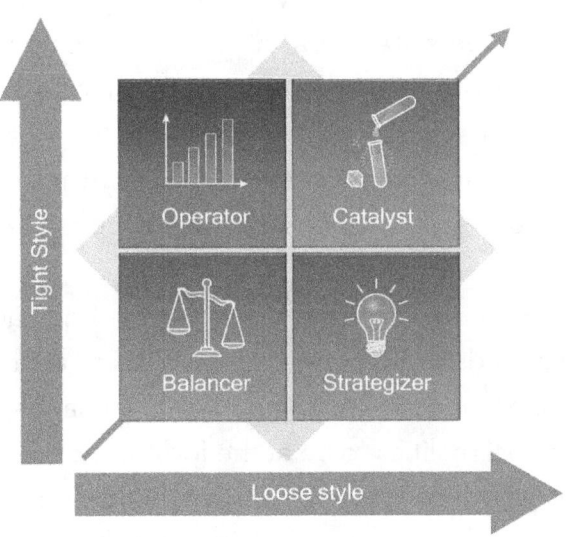

Operators have a preference for the 'tight' approach to leadership

An operator is likely to manage, lead, and implement change in a way that reflects a preference for dealing with tangible operational realities where visible improvements can be made. If you feel this is your nearest archetype, you may deal with change and uncertainty in a way that reflects a preference for operational, controlled, and perhaps tactical behaviors. You may seek to manage complexity by breaking problems down into smaller parts and addressing each separately or in turn. You might seek plans for immediate action and look for quick wins rather than spend time deliberating on the bigger picture or strategic issues; these may feel less critical to you, especially when things are ambiguous. This style has its place, especially in a more stable environment that requires operational improvements rather than any significant change. However, our experience is that such an environment is rarely experienced in modern organizations.

It is important to point out, though, that the operational aspect of change is incredibly important. Without the right emphasis on implementation and some eye for details, change may never really get off the ground. A change process dominated by someone with a strategizer preference (see below) might be interesting and even radical, but without some operator input, it could stall at the first hurdle because it is entirely unrealistic.

Some leaders feel that realism holds them back and that incremental thinking holds back change. Actually, there are stages in every process of change no matter how radical the change; some stages require operational realities to be at the forefront of our thoughts and actions. This is where an operational set of behaviors can really help. Pragmatism has an important place in any process of transformation, and the operator preference can reflect an inclination to be pragmatic rather than too idealistic.

The Strategizer

Strategizers have a preference for more 'blue sky' ways of thinking

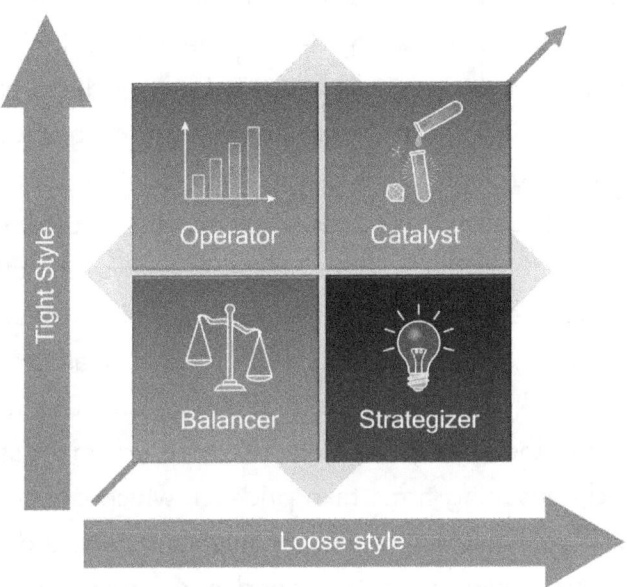

A strategizer may prefer innovation, transformational change, or radical change over more gradual or incremental change. Sometimes others feel strategizers are too strategic and don't focus enough on operational reality, day-to-day results, continuous improvement opportunities, or quick wins.

If you think this archetype is closest to your own preferences, you are likely to be in your element when there is a need for attention to the bigger picture, for more complete or total transformation with a vision or future end state in mind, than when smaller, immediate improvement is needed. You may feel most able to create value when the scope for innovation is very significant and when you can conceptualize a radically different future for a unit or a business. You may be less able to address immediate operational requirements or to generate quick wins within shorter time frames. You may also feel dragged into too much tedious operational detail and process when there is little opportunity to focus on the bigger picture.

Interestingly, those in strategy development roles don't always have strategizer preferences. They may actually be very detail oriented and analytical, with an inclination to create strongly data-driven, detailed long-term plans with high levels of confidence, rather than use a more intuitive or conceptual style. The term "strategizer" thus does not imply that those in strategic planning or strategic analysis functions always show the strategizer preference. Indeed, to their surprise, they may identify more with operators, who prefer highly analytical and structured ways of thinking, less like natural innovators. This may also say something about the slightly linear analytic methods many strategy professionals and consulting firms take pride in, which genuine strategizers, especially those with entrepreneurial leanings and a degree of risk propensity, may not always feel they need in making business decisions.

If we now review the seven areas of cultural orientation that create common cultural dilemmas within organizations, it becomes clearer how the role of the catalyst is important in reconciling them:

Change: Should we build on existing practices or do something radical?

Change-agile practices require us to manage today's operational business—even to make operational improvements—while also delivering more fundamental strategic transformation.

Planning: Should we focus on detailed plans to reach this quarter's number or on building the five-year strategy?

Change-agile practices require leaders to create tomorrow today. In other words, leaders need to deliver the results they have promised while also planning exponential future growth, driving more systemic changes to the business's operating model. This is not an easy feat and might require parallel running of today's organization with one or even several new potential operating models for the future. Change-agile business planning requires the ability to work with a variety of both short- and long-term scenarios.

Risk: Should we minimize risk or maximize returns?

Organizations that take no risks are less likely to get strong results in a VUCA world, which moves fast. Risk and reward go together, and the challenge of leadership is to manage risk well without slowing down growth. Shareholders don't want to sacrifice earnings growth, but neither do they want to be too exposed to risk.

Product development: Should we have standardized global products or customize them locally?

Customers expect the best of both from corporations—global scale, global know-how, and world-class quality plus local intelligence and relevance to their needs wherever they are. If they go to a branded hotel, they expect to experience the same essence of the brand anywhere in the world. They also expect to experience something suited to the local environment and of the local culture or region they are in.

Working environment and infrastructure: Should we use structured working practices and operational metrics or allow people freedom to decide what works best for them?

A business that has embraced change agility has appropriate operational tools, processes, metrics, and procedures to help employees get the job done brilliantly and also allows a degree of freedom or autonomy. Employees need the right blend of structure and freedom to serve customers well. In particular, agile workplaces allow freedom of movement, use of office space, and time while also creating structured ways of using workplace facilities.

Decision making: Should we make decisions through a hierarchical process or give people room to make mistakes and experiment?

Change-agile organizations and leaders know which decisions need to be made very slowly with the input of their most experienced people and which decisions can be made more quickly right at the sharp end. Organizations that require senior management's sign-off on purchases of trivial items, for example, are unlikely to be great places to work or very quick to respond to employees' or customers' needs. More bureaucratic (or, indeed, altogether indecisive) organizations may have a very high need for control, which in a VUCA world not only slows them down but also stifles creativity.

Priority setting: Should our priorities be driven by the bottom line or by our corporate values?

This is a false polarity, really, as the role of a leader is to generate great returns for shareholders and also to contribute to the core purpose of the organization. Most organizations today have compelling mission statements and values they espouse. It is time for more corporate leaders to buy into such purpose and live the values while also achieving their financial targets. In the world's most admired companies, the two go hand in hand in the long run. CEOs and senior leaders cannot declare victory unless they win in a purposeful, ethical way.

BITE-SIZED CASE:

VP of Sales for SE Asia

The Scenario: A Vice President of Sales for SE Asia in a Global Business Services Company

A vice president of sales creates a radical proposal for a new client in Indonesia and will present the proposal for internal approval from the corporate office in Singapore. She has not taken the time to engage the right people in Singapore or in the global HQ in London about the risks and benefits of her proposed solution for the new client.

This client solution will create significant change in the way the company works. It requires a different pricing model from the global one currently used, and it requires a different resourcing approach that uses a local partner in Indonesia to get much of the work done. In the VP's view, this is not very high risk and will help the company gain an important foothold in a major new market where demand will grow in the long term.

The solution was not approved. She should have thought more about the operational and internal realities that would have allowed it to be creative and feasible internally. Had she engaged her global colleagues and the regional team in Singapore much earlier, she might have found the right way to build the solution and to present it for internal approval.

While many executives in emerging markets are frequently frustrated by the weight of HQ bureacracy, they must remember that without backing from a large multinational and all its resources, they would be pretty much on their own in these markets, competing purely at a local level. There are considerable benefits to global scale and coordination combined with strong local ties. To win in emerging markets, these factors must be harnessed using several elements of agility.

Reconciling Cultural Dilemmas the Change-Agile Way

A sense of purpose helps to manage complexity as represented by cultural dilemmas, particularly when they impact organizational change. You can apply a common purpose to find creative ways to reconcile the dilemmas you face in your organization. The role of purpose is illustrated below.

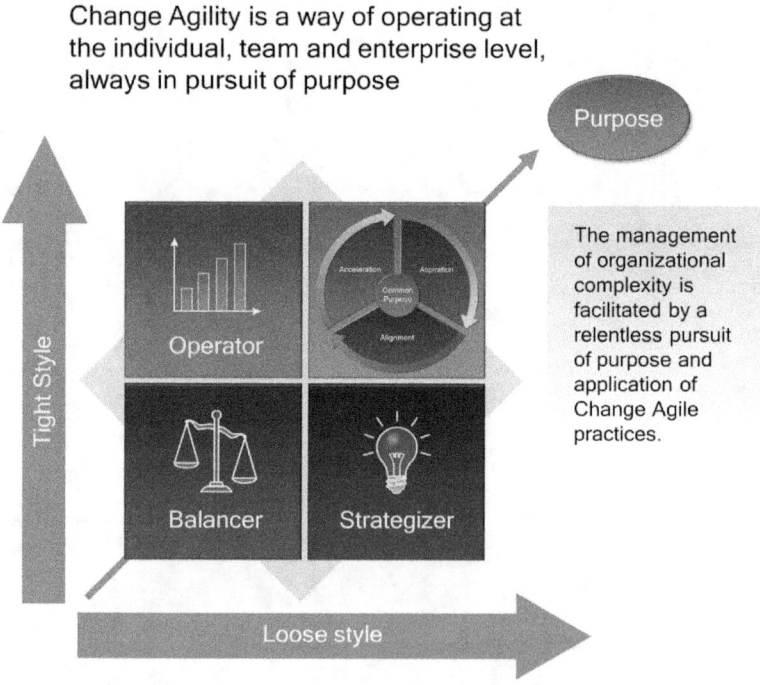

The role of purpose is to create a reference point for success so that different options or scenarios can be tested for viability and attractiveness. Shared purpose reframes and elevates the debate on key issues and decisions. It helps to keep us out of the "either-or"

level of compromise-based decision making and into a more opti-mized, "both-and" way of making and executing decisions.

The evidence from several industries and from the government sector suggests that what counts in today's environment is a relent-less focus on agility, which in our view is the definitive ingredient for longevity, excellence, or greatness in the twenty-first-century enter-prise. Companies need to be permanently agile, and their people should constantly work *in pursuit of purpose*. Companies must strive to build agile capabilities and pursue purpose to survive and thrive in uncertain times.

In the future, we may find that even companies like Google who appear to show many facets of change agility now, after being domi-nant in their markets for a while may grow stuck in their ways. Their strengths may well eventually become exaggerated, and this exposes them to extremely agile competitors in the future. Agility seems to erode as soon as market dominance is reached. Becoming the market leader in a sector is therefore just the start of the journey for truly winning companies in today's global business environment. Winning companies never declare victory, yet they always still celebrate suc-cess. That in itself is a bit of a paradox.

What should be self-evident from our descriptions of archetypes is that every team, especially a leadership team, includes people with different preferences. This can influence in quite fundamental ways how the team behaves together and how, from a leadership point of view, others experience the team—particularly during times of uncertainty or change. It is also possible that whole departments (or, indeed, organizations) demonstrate biases toward one arche-type or another. Some clients and even sectors we work with have a very operational preference, preferring to focus on quarterly results, metrics, and things they can do to "turn the needle" today. In general, we find that some business functions may naturally lean toward one preference or another, particularly on the "loose-tight" spectrum.

It is worth asking yourself where you, your team, your function or department, and your organization are on the spectrum, which success factors of change agility you demonstrate, and where you have important capability gaps.

Accelerating Change in Pursuit of Purpose

As we discussed earlier, change is often depicted as a painful journey or a trajectory from an "as-is" point to a future "to-be" point—consisting of an ending, a transition state, and a new beginning. It is often shown as a curve or a series of steps that eventually bring about transformational change.

Change Management practice seeks to reduced disruption due to change.

Change Agility seeks to remove fragility altogether as benefits are always temporary and context is permanently shifting

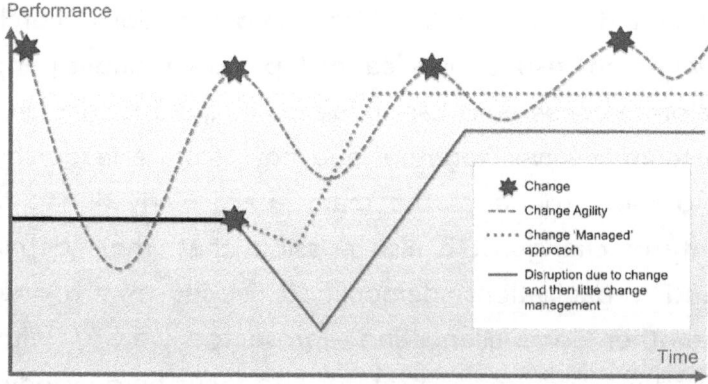

These models all have significant merits, especially for relatively small-scale programs or a change that is easily defined. (The traditional change curve and contrasting agile change curve are shown again for you to consider afresh.) Change of this kind creates temporary disruption that needs to be managed. Managing the disruption well reduces the performance lost due to change. Seeing change this way, however, is a fundamentally fragile state of mind and way of being in the first place. In this mental frame, change is treated like a source of disruption, something to be managed. In reality, change is the reason all companies and organizations exist. Whether it is to find raw materials and transform them into products that improve or transform consumers' lives or to create public services that do the same, corporate leaders are in the business of transformation. It's their reason for existence. So why do we still believe, after decades of research and practice in organization development, that change is an existential threat? Why do we assume that resistance to change is, in fact, the natural reaction of employees?

Our experience suggests that many more employees are naturally open to being agents of change than are change resisters if they are treated with the respect they deserve—as genuine architects of the future with some influence on the decisions that help make change possible. While the classical change management models are useful for thinking about effective navigation of individual change initiatives, overall they do not seem to capture the benefits that a truly engaged approach to change can bring at an enterprise level.

Perhaps we can overcome or minimize the usual shocks and disruption from change evident in nonagile organizations. The model we propose is the "spiral of value." It is created in a whole organization in which change is part of work life and where everyone plays a role in leading and managing change, not just those in leadership positions. In such a model, the impermanence of our work and our current state is liberating and normal, because it creates *room to grow as a result of change*. In this view, change is not necessarily to be feared as a source of insecurity.

The Spiral of Value

Experience tells us that change is less a linear or continuous curve and more of a spiral of value creation and value destruction as depicted below.

The Spiral of Value

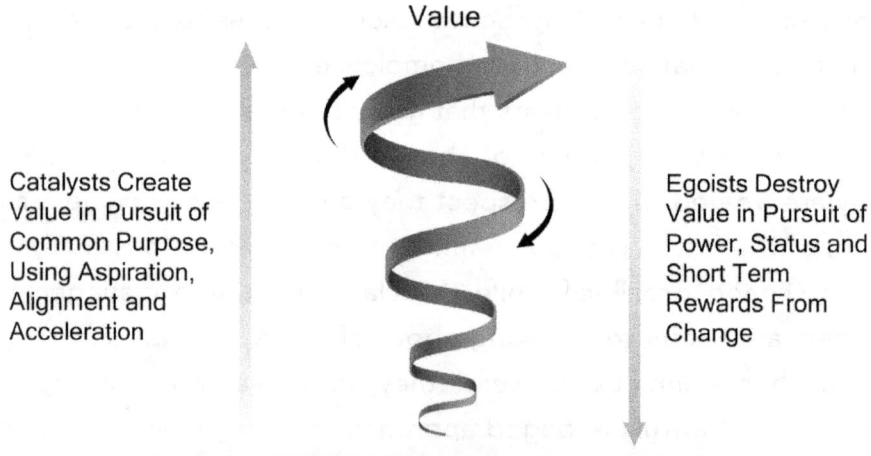

Value

Catalysts Create Value in Pursuit of Common Purpose, Using Aspiration, Alignment and Acceleration

Egoists Destroy Value in Pursuit of Power, Status and Short Term Rewards From Change

Change in organizations is multi-layered and if it is managed well it can create value. If managed poorly, by leaders following a purely personal agenda change can destroy value.

The spiral can be value creating or value destroying depending on the way leaders handle change. Each layer in the spiral (representing a layer of organizational change) requires constant reinforcement of *aspiration*, continual *alignment*, and practical *acceleration* to harness change and manage complexity (which often comes in the form of tough dilemmas).

The role of catalysts—those who are best able to reconcile cultural and organizational dilemmas—is significant in the pursuit of common purpose. Common purpose transcends specific objectives or financial goals for a particular strategy or change initiative. An egoist, by contrast, destroys value in pursuit of domination and personal status. Psychological research shows that many or most of us can find ourselves enacting an egoist state of being while in leadership positions. Many people in organizations certainly do pursue status or their own agendas at the expense of others, which can not only destroy value but also an organization's sense of shared purpose.

Were we to profile psychologically those corporate executives who have made front-page news in the last ten years for the wrong reasons and ended up being punished or imprisoned, we may find that the biggest obstacle to their effectiveness as leaders was their own extreme need for power or fame at all costs. Research suggests that some executives who derail in this way are likely to have very complex, narcissistic personalities showing a combination of extremely high self-importance and deep insecurity. A highly egotistical leader's long-term effect on an organization is a downward spiral of toxic emotions, erosion of trust, and loss of effectiveness.

The change agility model, with purpose at its core, can help organizations manage the "dark side" of leadership that some people may be vulnerable to. Leaders with a strong dark side to their personalities can create emotional toxicity in teams, and those with fragile-but-big egos can treat change as an opportunity to manipulate others for personal gain. Although people with this kind of personality are best not in leadership positions in the first place, the reality is that people sometimes become leaders because of their technical or commercial acumen alone. In corporate environments those who seek power tend to seek positions of power. An agile cultural context will help people with self-serving tendencies to look closely at their own sources of motivation. In an agile cultural context, egoists tend not to last very long or they are forced to serve an enterprise purpose and to treat change as an opportunity to serve the greater good.

Each layer in the spiral of value requires constant use of the change agility success factors and ongoing reconciliation of leadership dilemmas. The spiral is a model for change that is dynamic and highly iterative in nature, which we believe better reflects the way change occurs and is experienced at scale in complex and highly matrix-driven organizations. Different types of change in a change-agile organization are layered upon each other in complex ways to create an overall sense of movement toward a higher purpose. The journey is not linear or very predictable. Sometimes you may even go backward (down the spiral) as some things you try will actually fail. This is to be expected. However, with clarity of purpose, people who feel connected to the cause and to each other in pursuit of it, and the commitment to take action even in uncertain situations, we increase our likelihood of progression up the spiral.

There are at least three key implications for leadership of change:

First, change is not linear or simple but complex and cyclical, so leadership also needs to take into the account the natural complexity and chaos implicit within change.

Next, change in large organizations has several layers and sources. These may be impossible to measure or even understand if we are talking about a global enterprise with hundreds of thousands of employees or a large government service serving millions of citizens. This principle requires leaders to be humble about how they view their roles as architects and enablers of change in the short term. (Many leaders who have attended courses on leadership are unfortunately now steeped in delusional optimism about how easy it will be to bring about their visions for the future if they use change management methods well.)

Third, catalysts in organizations serve a purpose external to themselves, not an internal vision. In serving this purpose, they are able to put the needs of the organization and its stakeholders first. This especially goes for leaders. Leaders who serve only their own needs for power and status or simple financial reward tend to be toxic influences in the workplace. The egoists, such as those who have led various famous American institutions into collapse in recent years, need to be identified early and counseled about the integrity of their behavior.

Although examples like Lehman Brothers and the plethora of other recently collapsed institutions are obvious, we are concerned that similar dynamics exist in many organizations; they are just not at the point of total collapse. The implication is that the world's investors, employees, and consumers are not receiving from many—perhaps most—large institutions the kind of economic and social value that they should rightly expect from well-managed, agile institutions.

The spirit in which we have arrived at and share this model for organizational change is not to attempt academic completeness or to prescribe a detailed methodology for leaders. This is a guidebook, not an instruction manual or standard operating procedure for change. We provide the spiral of value to stimulate your own thinking and help you start conversations with those you work with about whether the changes in your organization are creating or destroying value—and why. Do people feel the organization operates on a virtuous spiral or a negative spiral? Your conversations should raise important questions that can only help you raise the bar on your performance such that you and other leaders around you create a spiral of value.

Change agility is an individual, team, and organizational capability that enables constant fulfillment of core purpose by harnessing the positive features of change on which people thrive. Agility is therefore the key enabler of sustained competitive advantage, and we also believe it can be a definitive feature of organizational effectiveness in a VUCA world. To be agile, an organization must build aspiration, reconcile cultural dilemmas, create deep alignment, and accelerate into the future.

You need to transcend the boundaries of a typical, fixed, three-to-five-year strategy enshrined in endless spreadsheets and PowerPoint decks put together by very smart MBAs in your organization. You need to have these plans and presentations, but in the end, winning is about having a workforce that works as one toward a collective purpose. If people are collectively able to deal with VUCA, then you are already partway toward winning.

Clearly, strategic choices do count. Our hunch, though, is that some CEOs spend too much time worrying about strategic choices on an analytical level with small groups of advisors. CEOs would benefit from spending at least as much time building an agile organization and developing people to make the right choices for themselves in critical cultural moments of truth.

At a human level, a clearly articulated strategy enables mission fulfillment; it is not an end in itself. It is the human dimension of change our clients find most challenging, not the analytical side. There is an army of hardworking, well-trained, and ambitious people in strategy consulting firms with MBAs who can help solve analytical problems for CEOs. But amid the realities and complexities of organizational life, honest, open, and constructive conversation becomes the most important leadership tool of them all. Leadership is less about solving problems or driving change in a linear, analytical way than it is about the constant reconciliation of dilemmas across large, networked organizations. Leaders who are able to orchestrate and facilitate the right conversations at the right time to achieve this reconciliation are those who catalyze transformational and strategic change.

The edge is a risky place to be: but can any organisation afford not to spend some time there?

—Arthur Battram

INDUSTRY EXAMPLE:

Ethical Practices in Pharmaceutical Industry

The Scenario: Britain's biggest pharmaceutical company, GlaxoSmithKline's stated commitment to stop paying doctors to promote its drugs.

In 2013, several media channels reported GlaxoSmithKline's public commitment to ending payments to doctors for recommending its drugs to other doctors at medical conferences. Sir Andrew Witty, GSK's chief executive, said that pharmaceutical firms must end the standard practice of paying independent doctors to promote drugs and sought to put patients' interests first. GSK acknowledged that when it gives information to doctors about its medicines, it must be done clearly, transparently, and without any perception of conflict of interest. GSK is demonstrating that it is putting patients' interests where they belong: at the heart of the business. This is an example of "both-and" thinking. Applying the loose-tight preference dimension we described in our model, it represents working to maximize profits *and* to be patient-centric, not one *or* the other. GSK pursues this dual purpose by hiring doctors openly and directly, being more transparent in the way they engage the medical profession to promote products. Drug companies all need to work with the medical profession to reach patients—they just need to do it *in the right way*. Embracing this mind-set requires cultural transformation of the sector.

BITE-SIZED CASE:

CEO of a Global Technology Manufacturing Company

The Scenario: Turnaround of a Global Technology Hardware Manufacturing Company

The highly qualified and intelligent CEO of a global tech hardware company came on board after several decades of family ownership. He was a seasoned CFO from the private equity industry who had provided financing for companies looking to grow. His analytical skills were very sharp. However, he had taken on a very serious turnaround challenge. He needed to revitalize the culture of innovation in the company and turn its financial performance around.

For two years, he pushed the company's global sales force for pipeline increases, especially in emerging and high-growth markets around the world, while slashing operating costs. This temporarily boosted the share price. However, he failed to engage the organization fully around the need for a systemic cultural change. Distributors' warehouses were stuffed with products that weren't selling through in retail outlets. There was serious discontent in the organization and a belief that the CEO was cynically boosting the value of his own lucrative share options. Through several disconnected, tactical downsizings, the heart and soul of the company was gradually being lost. The company was eventually broken up and partly sold, a shadow of its former self.

A CEO's pursuit of short-term results without clarity of purpose led to a downward spiral in performance. This was a transformation that failed. The company's high credibility with loyal customers was broken. Many very good people left to pursue careers at companies where they were able to realize their potential.

Creating the Climate for Change – the Change Agility Wheel

Change Agility Success Factors

Each area of capability can be measured with 3 sub components:

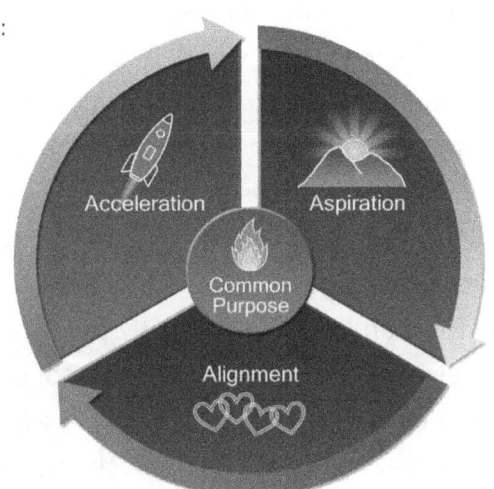

Aspiration
- Purposeful
- Integrative
- Inclusive

Alignment
- Constructive
- Creative
- Versatile

Acceleration:
- Responsive
- Adaptive
- Resilient

Since change should be a spiral of value and transformation in organizations, we have represented the change process as a wheel of growth that helps to move people up the spiral. To create a successful climate for change in your team or organization, it is possible as a leader to be engaged in activity in every part of this wheel. At some points in your own leadership journey, you may find yourself working much more on building aspiration for yourself and others—clarifying mission and purpose—than on making things happen on the ground. At other times, you may focus much more on acceleration of outcomes, getting things done, generating practical wins, and helping people to overcome obstacles.

It is helpful at any point in your own work as a leader to engage in activity that generates alignment with and between others so they can collaborate effectively. One of the biggest barriers to successful change agility is the chronic presence of negative emotion, which can be toxic for an organization. Cynicism, unhealthy internal competition, criticism that is not constructive: these are signs that alignment does not exist.

The change agility wheel illustrates the role each success factor for change agility plays in creating a suitable climate for change. The wheel is built on our model of integrated, holistic change that is anchored in your context and draws on every kind of human energy—mental, emotional, physical, and inner (or spiritual)—at all levels in a dynamic way. A climate for change is fostered in a team, a business unit, or whole organization when leaders constantly seek to utilize all of these energies in themselves and others, not just parts of them. This kind of climate is not only more change ready; it is also more likely to result in innovation and renewal in every sense—without the need for crisis.

For decades, our society has assumed that renewal happens through crisis—"never waste a good crisis" being an old adage. However, it is surely time to move on from waiting for renewal to occur through crisis and to create organizational cultures that naturally seek out constant redefinition and renewal. This is the essence of a climate for change, in our view. It is not just about readiness, actually. It is about curiosity and hunger for growth. You can create this kind of engaged, change agile-climate using the kinds of practices we describe below.

As you read through the list, think also about other things you feel you can do to help build a climate in which change is not seen as a threat but something natural and to be expected.

Build Aspiration

This success factor is about creating shared aspiration for change as positive and for it to lead further up the spiral of transformation toward value and purpose:

Articulate and reinforce common purpose to support change

Clarify the core purpose for the organization, your team, and yourself. Define clear short- and long-term goals that are consistent with this purpose. Do this even in the absence of a strategy, a clear "strategic blueprint," or end state to work toward.

Seek out and integrate different points of view throughout any change process

Take on board as many different perspectives on the critical dilemmas that affect change by engaging in open and honest conversations about change.

Overcome personal or cultural biases and help others to do the same.

Promote inclusiveness and diversity of thought in conversations and actions

Promote unity across internal silos and cultures in the context of the changes taking place.

Appreciate the roles that different cultural perspectives play in informing how change can be implemented.

Build aspiration in the organization in a way that exploits difference.

Create Alignment

Build appetite for any kind of change through dialogue and emotional connection:

Coach others to be constructive in how they engage with each other

Encourage creative conflict rather than artificial harmony. Ask probing questions and bring together people with naturally different views.

Provide opportunities for both support and challenge in small groups, allowing peers to coach each other through change.

Encourage creativity at all points in the change process

Get data from several, seemingly conflicting sources to understand external drivers for change and build shared understanding of these drivers.

Use the intuition and experience in the organization as well as rigorous analysis to create deep insight that then helps to manage complexity.

Demonstrate versatility at all key turning points in change

Promote change networks and communities rather than just work through traditional structures.

Apply controls, high-quality risk management, and robust decision-making processes to manage change while also creating space for mistakes and learning to occur.

Enable Acceleration

Drive momentum and a sustained response to collective enterprise challenges so that the change is visible and generates clear wins:

Demonstrate responsiveness in practical ways that add value to the business

Use both formal processes and informal methods to take action and achieve goals, breaking the rules at times within the boundaries of the organization's values.

Be prepared to make visible sacrifices to pursue purpose.

Show adaptive behavior, not routinized behavior

Accommodate new information or needs of the organization throughout the process of transformation with regular checkpoints and reviews of progress.

Be prepared to change direction quickly if necessary without putting the overarching purpose at risk.

Reinforce resilience to support transformation at all levels

Check that people have the emotional capacity to learn by testing their will, mental toughness, and courage in damage-free environments.

Ensure that people are able to cope with high levels of sustained pressure and offer regular psychological "safety valves" so they can vent their frustrations and concerns without fear of judgment (as long as the spirit of this is to pursue collective purpose relentlessly).

We don't want to suggest that you can remove all personal risks or pressures inherent to working in a VUCA environment, and our intention in this guide is not to provide a detailed checklist of things to do at different "stages" in a change initiative. We offer more a holistic description of the behavior needed among leaders and throughout the process of transformation to ensure positive momentum. Clearly, the high-level concept does need to be translated into project plans, timelines, specific meetings, workshops, project activities, assessments, and processes that drive the momentum. It is our hope that the guidance on accelerating change serves to inform your choice of specific interventions to get the results you want within your context and according to your own timeline.

The timeline for changes inevitably shifts or evolves in line with circumstances. However, the principles you adopt to facilitate transformation serve as focal points, as psychological constants throughout the process of change. The table below outlines the operating principles that leaders and managers of change can adopt throughout the cycle of transformation to enable effective execution. Each success factor for change agility can be applied at every stage in an organizational change process to create shared aspirations for the change, to generate alignment to change, and to accelerate progress toward a common purpose. Use the key success factors of change agility throughout the change process. Engage head, heart, hands, and spirit to catalyze the process of change.

Change Success Factor	Key Operating Principles
Aspiration	• Define the aspiration for the change that relates to the organization's core purpose or mission • Work relentlessly toward this aspiration • Draw in as many different perspectives and diverse opinions as you can throughout the process of change
Alignment	• Create emotional alignment to foster collaboration during change • Help people learn from each other's different and diverse experiences • Overcome tensions that arise from organizational complexity through reconciliation rather than confrontation

Acceleration	• Enable acceleration to secure practical wins • Encourage appropriate risks and devolve responsibilities for implementing change to the lowest possible level in the organization • Push for results from change at every stage, not just at the end of the change

Change requires leaders to engage the minds, the hearts, the physical energies, and the spirits ofthe people needed to make change happen as outlined below. The usual corporate presentations with facts and figures about the "business case," the "program office," and other very sensible project management methods do not suffice to embed change in a complex human system. You are dealing with people, so engage every aspect of their being and the results will be exponentially better. Even those who are negatively impacted by change in some way are more likely to feel they can contribute if they see the purpose behind it and how they can make a difference. They are more likely to put aside their own personal anxieties until they are properly addressed, at least for a while, to help others and be constructive—if you include them in the process of meaningful, authentic engagement.

Engage people at every level with every type of energy

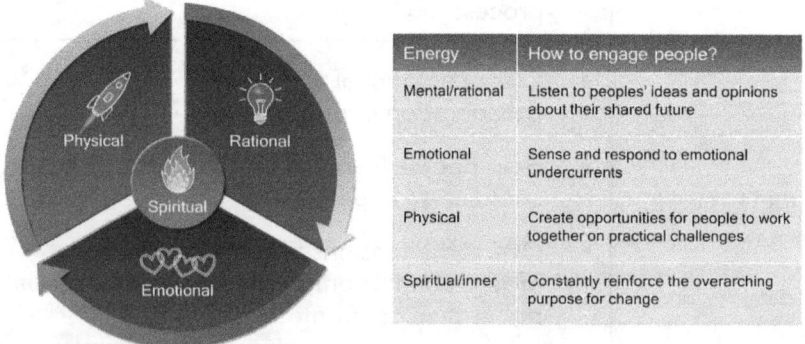

Energy	How to engage people?
Mental/rational	Listen to peoples' ideas and opinions about their shared future
Emotional	Sense and respond to emotional undercurrents
Physical	Create opportunities for people to work together on practical challenges
Spiritual/inner	Constantly reinforce the overarching purpose for change

We hope that the approach we share here doesn't come across as a "one size fits all" method for organizational change or as a process with a series of well-defined steps you should take. There are other methods that treat the leadership of change like this, and we do not intend to replicate them. They tend to adopt quite similar patterns that start with an as is" and move an organization toward a "to be." In cultural terms, we are not convinced that there ever can really be such a thing as a "to-be" state in a VUCA world—there is only a culture in constant need of improvement and greater change capacity.

It may be more appropriate to think of cultural transformation as a "less-of" and "more-of" process of collective development than a kind of project process that goes "from x to y." Beware of any approach to change that does not allow you to decide the right approach for your organization or your own project, based on your own context. We provide some basic principles for you to apply as you see fit in your business to accelerate change, not a programmatic methodology with a series of steps in neatly compartmentalized boxes. That's not really how the real world works—not now. And perhaps it never has. It could be that much of the frustration leaders have experienced with change comes from the illusion of control some project-managed change methods have created around managing large-scale organizational change.

It is no coincidence that huge professional services companies that talk up the value of simplistic change management methods also tend to sell large systems-integration programs or operational and business process transformation of some kind. It is unlikely that these organizations would actually confess the possibility of zero return on investment on change due to the fragility of traditional change management methods and, indeed, of any transformation initiative. The work required to build a change-ready organization correlates with any successful strategic change, and hopefully our stance is clear: change readiness is a major undertaking in its own right, not just a tactical add-on to other programs.

Change agility is a departure from the "Mary Poppins" approach to change in which a "spoonful of sugar makes the medicine go down"—with change management practices as the sugar. Leadership of change is not sugarcoating for the otherwise bitter pill of change. This is a paradigm that agile organizations strive to discard. Our sense is that employees at all levels naturally mistrust the Poppins approach anyway and recognize a bitter pill for what it is. Rather, in a change-agile climate, people prefer to feel like adults who can take difficult medicine if they feel it is for the greater good (or, indeed, for their own good). There is a dividend from treating employees at all levels equitably, fairly, and with respect as active partners in change, not just recipients of it.

INDUSTRY EXAMPLE:

Outsourcing and Shared Services Implementation

The Scenario: Any Organization Contemplating Outsourcing Business Processes or Implementing Shared Services

Implementing outsourcing or shared services requires the right approach to managing a complex psychological change, possibly in several countries. An organization in Asia has made several attempts to transform its back office and IT capabilities across several different subsidiaries where there has been much duplication of effort and waste of resources.

Although on paper the change appeared to have a strong business case and many other organizations had done it, the level of internal resistance to it, especially at senior levels, was hugely underestimated. For any shared services or outsourcing program to be successful, several human factors must be considered at every stage from exploring initial feasibility to implementation. The team leading the program needs a very high level of emotional agility. Its ability to read the cultural and political signals to help transition and transform business support functions requires very strong leadership and change skills.

Turning Negative Energy into Positive Energy for Change

In a change-agile organization, "resistance" to change is treated differently than it might be in an organization that only uses more traditional change management methods. A great deal depends on how the change is presented to its people rather than on the actual nature of the change or outcomes in question.

The usual view of resistance to change we encounter in organizations is that people are naturally resistant until they are able to see "what's in it for them." This is to be expected in organizations that have not worked on creating a sense of common purpose. Shared purpose transcends day-to-day ways of working or specific functional responsibilities. If people feel inspired by the overarching purpose that drives the organization in a certain direction, then any resistance is more likely to reflect their pride in the good work that is already being done and their concern for the health of the organization. Whatever form resistance takes, it is feedback—and feedback is a gift!

Here are some principles to reflect on and apply:

- Change agility harnesses resistance to create even more momentum

- Open resisters care enough to resist openly

- Engage and listen to resisters

- Harness resisters' energy to create even more change

- Differentiate between wilful or tacit resistance and genuine concern

Much organization development research has shown the importance of participation and involvement in change—not as a means to overcome or prevent resistance, but as a way to lead change authentically, really listening to and understanding different views to arrive at solutions. It is striking how much change management seems to happen purely in service of a particular leader's vision (or that of a select few) rather than in service of a collective, shared aspiration with a truly human component.

Visionary leadership can in fact encourage resistance because there is something fundamentally disempowering about a vision that belongs only to one individual or a small group rather than an organization as a whole. Visionary leadership seeks to overcome resistance or work around it. So many (indeed, most) models of change leadership insist on the need for leaders to have (or articulate) visions. This has the unintended consequence of building a parent-child relationship between those who lead change and those who are willing participants in it at best—and at worst, unwilling subjects of autocratic change (albeit with the sugarcoated delivery we discussed earlier).

Change-agile leadership helps create shared identity in an organization so that everyone feels change is for them to own and to drive for the greater good. A change-agile leader is not the sole owner or conceptualizer of a vision for the organization but can own the process for building a truly inspiring shared aspiration. Agile leaders seek out points of resistance through the constant process of engagement, demonstrating their curiosity and harnessing the diversity of reaction rather than attempting to crush it. Curiosity helps to turn resistance into dialogue.

As we noted, those who are openly resistant may be so out of concern rather than resistance for its own sake. Agile leaders seek to understand and then address such concerns, turning resistance from a negative energy source—a drain on performance—into a positive source of energy, a positive performance spiral. Leaders who treat genuine and heartfelt concern as resistance are quickly derailed when the tide turns or circumstances are less than benign. Those who resist openly and on the basis of their convictions can become champions for change if their feedback and feelings can be voiced and are acknowledged rather than opposed or avoided.

Understand authentic concern through dialogue. Differentiate concern from resistance. See the signs and manage accordingly:

Characteristics of Resistance	Characteristics of Authentic Concern
Personal	Objective
Emotional	Sincere and heartfelt
A source of threat to a change process	A source of feedback and information
A sign of disengagement	A sign of care for the organization
Selfishly motivated	Intended to prevent mistakes
Detrimental to achieving an outcome	Helps achieve a better outcome
Should be carefully "handled" or overcome	Should be treated as serious input
Slows things down	Creates opportunity to reflect

It is clear that some are simply not equipped to be positive ambassadors for change. Some may even desire to terrorize the organization and its leadership during times of change. These are cynics and natural detractors who may never be able to embrace the spirit of the organization. They do exist. The right thing to do from a leadership perspective is not to avoid this reality but to face up to it and determine how to handle those without the raw material to contribute to the creation of a winning culture even when they actually deliver strong business results.

For handling fundamentally culturally misaligned people, change agility requires empathy coupled with objectivity. Finding and removing major sources of genuine internal drag, negativity, or toxicity in an organization while supporting those whose intent is positive and whose capabilities are aligned is part of the art of leadership in a VUCA world. Be very careful about becoming too dependent on results-oriented people who do not share the organization's values but are good at certain tasks. Ultimately, they become problems through the atmosphere they create unless they are coached to live the organization's values.

One global professional services firm we know has a team of fifty people in Asia for embarking on a radical journey of expansion in the region. One of the senior management team members never attends management meetings, off-site meetings, or company gatherings for staff. He has one client he has been servicing for several years with some success, and it is the firm's biggest source of revenue and profit in Asia. However, his impact on the rest of the team and reticence to contribute to leadership of the firm makes him more of a risk to sustained growth than an asset.

The firm has struggled to find a solution, because he has found self-serving ways to control the relationship with the one large client.

The other leaders have realized that this individual might well put the firm's expansion strategy at risk if he chooses to leave the organization and take this client relationship with him. The client revenue stream is, after all, an important source of cash flow as the firm seeks to expand. What was really required in this scenario was more collaboration at this particular client across the team from the outset—and certainly more agility from other senior leaders in identifying how to integrate this individual properly into the organization or let him go at the right time—before he felt able to hold them all for ransom.

Lone wolves are a common phenomenon in professional services firms, and with them can come the blessings of strong productivity contributions—and risks in the form of isolation or extreme internal competition. These lone wolves need to be strongly counseled and coached to behave appropriately according to the values of a professional firm. Such characters are usually only ever temporary sources of value creation rather than contributors to a firm's real legacy or external reputation.

As a business leader, you simply can't afford to have people in the boat that you cannot trust to do their very best help to make it go faster—and in the right direction. When you do discover a serious source of drag, you must act on your instincts with decisiveness, respect for the individuals or groups concerned, and, of course, authenticity in service of the organization. It is important that you make tough decisions about people in the organization with the highest possible purpose in mind. If you must make changes to your team because you don't have the right people in the "boat," then do it thoughtfully and have an appropriate plan to manage the transition. Impulsive or reactive actions very rarely work out well in constructing your team. Building a team needs to be done mindfully rather than too opportunistically, exercising conscious choice. Hiring or promotion decisions that you later regret are often those you make too quickly with an urgent need in mind, totally opportunistically and without the right behavioral data.

The challenge of change is partly, therefore, about helping to build a climate in which change agility is promoted and nurtured—where aversion to change is actually managed such that people maximize the energy they have for change. It is apparent to us that people in organizations are weary of change, partly because it has been led and managed badly or haphazardly in the past. Restructures frequently come out of the blue and seem to have no relation to any mission (or indeed strategy). Leaders talk the talk of mind-set and behavioral change but don't always walk the walk themselves. We have been engaged in development programmes in which – despite our efforts to prevent this - senior leaders attempt to coerce or even, in subtle ways, to bully people to embrace positive leadership concepts. This is itself counterproductive and extremely contradictory. Leadership with the positive, humanistic attributes we have described is best learned in the presence of such leadership. How leaders develop others and engage others in the process of change needs to be congruent with the kind of cultural norms which are seen to be healthy or desirable in the whole organization. We have even experienced an irascible Chief Marketing Officer publically berate and humiliate junior members of staff and external facilitators alike, during the course of an ambitious development programme for her senior team, when she felt things were not going the way she wanted. This completely undermined the whole process since the team – themselves senior managers – watched her unconsciously contradict all of the leadership principles being espoused during the programme, losing her temper and chastising various support professionals with an angry, accusatory tone. We have seen CEO's just delegate all of their leadership communication to an external consultant or coach who then adopts the center-stage position during critical meetings or events.

On one occasion we witnessed, a CEO's personal coach sit in the middle of a stage with the CEO and the executive team around him, as key issues were shared and discussed in a highly stage-managed way with a large group of leaders. The coach was acting as the orchestrator of the whole dialogue in such a way that it felt more like an entertaining chat-show than an authentic leadership conversation. This diluted the credibility of the whole process, even if it was great for the personal profile (and ego!) of the coach. The role of a responsible consultant or coach is to help the leader to do his or her job by facilitating, not taking on the mantle of leadership. The role of a speaking partner during change should be given, if at all, to other members of the senior executive team (like the HR leader, COO, or CFO), who many need to be prepared and supported by the facilitator to be able to do this confidently and effectively.

Naturally, some will show a degree of skepticism, especially perhaps those who have "seen it all before." "Learned taste aversion" is a psychological phenomenon in which people who eat or drink something that leads to a bad experience react to the substance in the future. For example, if someone experienced physical sickness after inebriation with a particular strong spirit, nausea can arise at the sight, smell, or even thought of having the same drink. Or a particular food may have made someone very ill. The same thing can happen with change. People can come to be averse even to the thought of workplace changes if they always result in negative consequences rather than positive results and personal growth.

We have constructed a simplified model for progressing from learned change aversion (as we think of it) to change agility. Typically, change management teaches us that we should seek to create change readiness before embarking on a change. Our view is that we can and must go further than readiness. We must go toward genuine hunger and active experimentation throughout the organization, seeking to stay ahead of the curve of change all the time. The energy people require to go from aversion to caution to readiness and then to agility—where they are highly energized—is outlined below.

The lowest energy level reflects *change aversion*. In this mode, people are not energized about the prospect of change and see at as negative. The next level is *caution*. In this mode, people are open but still wondering, "What's in it for me?" In the *ready* mode, there is plenty of energy for change and willingness to try things out. Many models of change stop at helping to move people from a state of cautious to ready. An *agile* state has heightened energy and a collective appetite for active learning. This is the kind of organizational culture that 3M has become known for: it encourages learning, experimentation, and innovation throughout the enterprise.

Levels of Energy for Change

Change Agile: People are curious, open, and enthusiastic to embrace collective leadership responsibility with an appetite for active experimentation.

Change Ready: People are energetic and willing to change because they understand why it is important to try out new ways of working.

Change Cautious: People are open to becoming more energized but want to see that there is something in it for them first. They are less eager to take the lead.

Change Averse: People are not energized about change. They are weary of change and have had negative experiences of it, so they perceive change as a threat that must be avoided or resisted.

To make it simple (and even fun) to think about where everyone is on the change response spectrum, we have put together a "change meter" to help leaders reflect on where they are, where people in their team may be, and where the organization as a whole might be. It supports the change archetypes nicely by showing the psychological levels of openness to change, which finally culminate in a catalyst approach. The change meter (below) can help you think about your level of energy for change and compare it to that of others. Big differences on the spectrum between people within a team or organization need to be managed carefully.

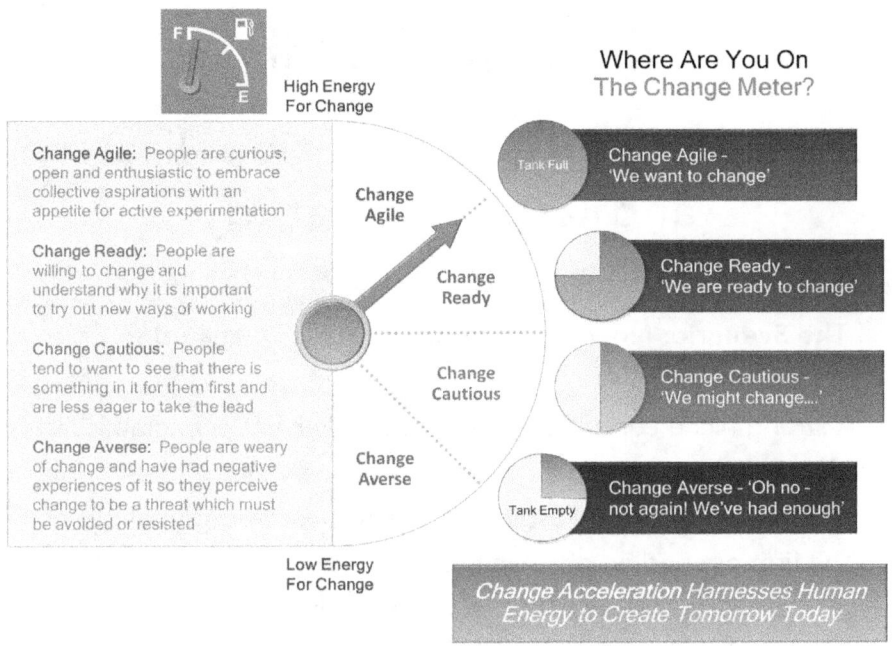

Where are you, your team, your department, and the whole organization on this spectrum? Especially if you lead a large number of people, you want them to have the energy to be change agile rather than just change ready. Readiness is too passive in a VUCA world: you and your organization need to be more than ready. You need to be disruptors of the status quo if it is inadequate and architects of change in your own right.

The change meter, of course, is just a quick tool for intuitive use (anytime, anywhere) rather than a diagnostic. Diagnostics are useful, but they are not very agile. If you can equip yourself and all those around you to be everyday diagnosticians, always looking for clues in the impact of your own behavior to enable higher performance, then your organization will need fewer external surveys and repetitive questionnaires to tell you what is already known and collectively ignored.

BITE-SIZED CASE:

Consulting Firm Internationalization and Growth Strategy

The Scenario: New Market Entry for a US Consulting Firm

A strong niche consulting practice already had very established offices and a presence in the United States, Europe, the Middle East, and Australia. Its aspiration was to be a truly global player. The firm opened an office in Singapore to cater more closely to clients in Asia. However, its appetite for the changes this would bring to the operating model was limited, and it sent someone to work in Asia without the right local connections or an understanding of the market. The firm was willing to experiment, but only using its usual approach to mature markets. The new office did not live up to expectations in the first two to three years and was closed down. Some years later, competitors are doing very well in the region, making healthy profits and winning new clients.

The company needed to be more creative in adapting to the needs of an emerging market for consulting services. It was simply too attached to its legacy and didn't have the right people on the ground to make its strategy work. If you embark on a new venture outside your traditional business, it is critical to adopt a change-agile approach. You need to be committed and open to the lessons of new markets for the whole organization. Don't try to lift and drop your existing business practices.

A common way in which organizations tend to kill change agility is to crush the natural drive, curiosity, and experimentation found in naturally agile people. In a financial services firm we know, a relatively new and very dynamic manager who was tasked with growing the practice footprint in frontier markets across Southeast Asia submitted plans for a new office in a recently liberalized Asian country to HQ in New York. He has spent a year engaged in discussions and submission of papers to several different internal stakeholders, corporate managers, and leaders in the United States.

During that time frame, competitors have set up shop in this rapidly expanding frontier for similar services. Frustration nearly led the manager to just give up and focus on other things, as he perceived that the appetite for change within the firm simply wasn't commensurate with his own. However, on reflection, he understood that sometimes the challenge of leadership is having to work in a less agile internal environment even when opportunities are staring a business in the face. He decided to maintain his focus and to hold his nerve while helping corporate staff in New York understand the realities of frontier markets.

More conservative, change-cautious or even change-averse cultures can be found in many professional services organizations, especially those whose ownership is distributed among several partners—sometimes hundreds or even thousands of them. Professional services firms such as those that practice law or accounting have not always been known for progressiveness or responsiveness to change. This attitude has shifted dramatically in the last ten years in many global professional services sectors, however, including global law firms and "Big Four" accountancies like PricewaterhouseCoopers or Deloitte, who are embracing more agile ways to go to market globally. They are even competing effectively in space that would have been difficult for them to contemplate some years ago, such as legal services and large-scale business process outsourcing.

As a regional leader in any sector, your own leadership challenge is to demonstrate a forward-thinking and open stance to new opportunities for growth. In a regional leadership role, you have to have faith in your ability to influence your organization's global and regional head offices to capitalize on these opportunities, to reconcile the various differing perspectives, even if you do not always manage to achieve exactly what you originally set out to achieve. We see too many regional executives become caught up in internal politics rather than work constructively towards optimized outcomes with their global counterparts. Equally we see too many global leaders ignore the need to be responsive to the needs of their colleagues in different regions. More mutual interest and the desire to serve a shared purpose can turn this kind of silo behavior into constructive behavior.

In the end, the manager in the example above relished the process of leading the organization through a structured thought process, presenting his ideas to the board using the right internal protocols to gain its support. He adopted a learning mind-set toward the firm's approach to evaluating propositions. He picked up new skills and tools for forecasting and analyzing return on investment using the firm's global business investment evaluation procedures. He saw this experience ultimately as a chance to learn how to influence the business so that when the time was right, he would successfully launch exciting ventures for the firm in growth markets.

His was a positive and optimistic approach to change in which the process of continuous learning and discovery is itself a source of personal inspiration, not just the outcomes of one's efforts. In a

VUCA world, things do not go our way much of the time, but we still need to create personal paths to success. An open, curious, and optimistic stance in line with a change-agile mind-set rather than a defeatist, obstinate, and pessimistic one may well lead you to places you could not have envisioned. Becoming overly attached to a plan for anything can make us blind to present realities and real opportunities.

BITE-SIZED CASE:

Leadership Team-Building for a Global Insurance Company in Asia

The Scenario: Driving Growth in the Asia Region

The leadership of a company had a new mandate and significant support for a major expansion drive in Asia, including China. Before embarking on any significant strategic or tactical ventures, the firm took some time together in a leadership off-site to which they invited all of their own direct reports. They felt it was very important to create a sense of shared purpose across the entire region and to agree on the kind of leadership behaviors needed to successfully grow the business in the face of fierce competition and unpredictable market conditions.

The leaders assessed their own levels of comfort with change and discussed their own styles. This yielded interesting insights. They then shared their insights across the whole team and identified the institutional strengths they could leverage. They also discussed how they would engage and align the rest of the organization within and outside Asia to support them on the long journey toward strategic growth. They made sure that every member of the leadership community in the whole region felt part of the growth plan, knew how they could contribute, and understood its importance to the core mission of the company globally. People were inspired by the meeting, and results in year one of the new growth plan showed it had been a worthwhile undertaking to bring people together for real dialogue.

CHANGE AGILITY IN ACTION

Cross-Sector Examples

A Change-Agile Island?

Singapore, a tiny, tropical island in the sea, has emerged as a serious force in several different global industry sectors in the space of a few decades. Just one major corporation within Singapore's stable of blue-chip companies is Sembcorp. Sembcorp is a world leader in energy, water, and marine solutions with operations on six continents. Sembcorp operates Jurong shipyard in Singapore, providing one-stop solutions in ship repair, shipbuilding, ship conversion, rig building, and offshore engineering and construction. It is a hive of activity and employment that delivers solid returns.

How has Sembcorp managed to do this in Singapore when a country such as the United Kingdom, with a heritage in marine engineering, has been shedding thousands of jobs and whole industries like shipbuilding, laying waste to whole communities? The answer is not simple or straightforward. The island city-state has shown aspiration and acceleration toward being an advanced, global city that can punch well above its weight as an economic player. This has required great agility from Singapore's various corporations in telecoms, aviation, engineering, construction and development, health care, technology, financial services, and investment.

For an island nation like Singapore to go from third world to first has required remarkable capacity for change and a big dose of courage. This agility needs to be retained for sustained success and growth. To this end and to its credit, the government has recognized that more attention is now needed to the emotional engagement and deeper well-being of Singapore's workforce. It is an increasingly important focal point for Singapore.

Winning in Developing Markets

The story of Tesco in China carries real lessons for the successful establishment of new businesses and especially internationalization strategies. With nearly 1.4 billion people, China is the world's biggest consumer market, but it is not an easy market for western multinationals to operate in without very good local connections and local know-how.

After struggling to generate strong returns in China, Tesco announced a joint venture with China Resources Enterprise, which has a much larger stores footprint than Tesco in China. In a somewhat similar vein, Carrefour pulled out from the Singapore market completely in 2012 after several years of attempting to compete with local retailers. It sold its 25 percent equity stake in a Middle East joint venture to its local partner, Majid Al Futtaim Group.

Global companies who are very strong in their home markets also have strong aspirations for growth in emerging markets in the Middle East and Africa—or in Asia. The complexities faced by multinational retailers in leading and growing profitable businesses overseas, however, often cause them to scale back their ambitions in emerging and frontier markets or pull out altogether. A change-agile approach to working in emerging markets, especially frontier markets (like Myanmar in Southeast Asia, only recently open for business with outsiders), requires multinationals to put in place the right organization locally. They must learn to exercise statecraft with governments and create alignment with local partners. Business expansion in regions such as Africa, Asia, and the Middle East requires tremendous agility from parent companies and their corporate leadership.

Change Agility Is the Key to Responsible Growth in the Fast-Moving Consumer Goods (FMCG) Industries.

Some of the biggest global consumer-goods corporations such as Procter & Gamble, Unilever, or Coca Cola are challenged to generate growth from the sale of consumer products while fulfilling their customer service objectives. These firms invariably state their commitment to sustainability and responsibility in their businesses practices. Many consumer companies manufacture and market food and beverage products which, if used in the wrong way or excessively, can damage human health or the natural environment.

One of the interesting developments in this area, especially visible at Unilever, is that the leaders of these companies have sought ways to avoid the trap of polarized thinking about this kind of dilemma. Unilever has stated very clearly on its corporate website that "sustainability is integral to how we do business." That is a bold and promising statement. Integrating CSR and sustainability into core business practices and the mission of the organization is critical to aligning the whole organization, its leadership, and operational priorities with a human agenda.

Harish Manwani, appointed as Unilever's global COO in 2011, spoke eloquently and convincingly at several different forums in his first two years about the need for leadership at Unilever to put consumers at the heart of the business, to drive growth responsibly, and to work toward a shared, collective purpose that is sustainable. The whole FMCG sector, including the fast food sector, is attempting to lead transformation in emerging markets where young populations of aspiring consumers are critical to their growth. Companies need a strong sense of purpose as they go about doing this.

Change Agility in the Global Travel Sector.

In the last thirty years, Changi Airport in Singapore has won countless awards and accolades for its quality of services, safety, and attractiveness to travelers. It has regularly been voted the world's best airport by consumer groups. This remarkable achievement is due to many things, not least of which is the relentless dedication and hard work of the airport's thousands of workers. The history of the airport's development included some tough choices, extensive land reclamation, and a huge infrastructure program.

To make it all happen, many aspects of change agility were mobilized. There was the power of aspiration to create a world-class airport for a global city. There was strong alignment between government and the private sector to mobilize the right investment and resources. There is acceleration toward the future with a relentless focus on quality execution and staying a step ahead of demand all the time. This is how Changi avoids the painful overcrowding and operational issues so visible in other airports.

The leadership of Emirates, voted the world's best airline in 2013, has also demonstrated to the world that with the right cross-sector collaboration that has deep social purpose and the power of aspiration, anything is possible. Emirates has helped to reinvent the United Arab Emirates into a tourist destination. It has invested in strong leadership capability, putting in place an organization that is ready to exploit market trends and customer preferences. A culture that is change ready has enabled Emirates to catapult to the top of the league in world airline rankings and performance, way ahead of many far more mature global competitors.

BITE-SIZED CASE:

CEO of an International Financial Institution in the Asia-Middle East-Africa Region

The Scenario: Corporate Transformation Program and Restructuring

"Sam," the regional CEO of a global bank, had an extremely complex leadership challenge. The institution was restructuring and transforming its whole business globally to radically reduce operating costs and overhead by 30 percent in light of significant financial pressures. Additionally, there was a strong push from HQ to implement a "culture change" requiring the whole bank to be much more customer-centric and more responsible than it had become in the previous five years.

Sam had to be part of this whole program of transformation, leading the implementation in his region and also contributing to it as a global leader in the bank. Of course, he also had to deliver exceptional growth in his region, given that some of the fastest-growing economic regions fell under his leadership. So, while restructuring and transforming the whole organization, he had to ensure the bank was not missing important opportunities for growth regionally. He had to find a way to deliver different and sometimes contrasting parts of his agenda concurrently...

Agile Leadership in Action

Sam decided that he needed to find a way to combine the global program for change and transformation with his regional strategy for growth. He could imagine real synergy for the region from capitalizing on lower operating costs across the bank, and he felt the organization could be more customer-centric.

He created a leadership action team of sixty top executives from across his region. This team became a vehicle for the leadership of change at a collective level. He formed a project group to help craft an appropriate transformation-and-growth strategy for the region, drawing on the various specialisms across the bank inside and outside the region. The HR director, head of strategy, and COO for the region all reported to him and became a steering group for this initiative. Together with the leadership action team, they created a pathway to profitable growth that was closely aligned with the global road map for change across the institution.

The leadership action team was split into several different multi-functional and cross-region work streams. These work-streams addressed different challenges associated with change in the region. What became critical for the whole process of change was to make key decisions and choices together regularly in light of market shifts and opportunities and to share the experiences of implementing changes. The group developed a "responsible growth charter" that contained its collective statement of purpose. It met virtually and face-to-face to ensure full engagement and deep alignment. This is the kind of approach that supports high performance and agility.

THREE KEY IDEAS TO TAKE AWAY FROM THIS SECTION

1 The ability to change, to adapt, in a VUCA world is a major contributor to performance. Change agility contributes to your personal results, to long-term competitiveness of your business, and to the growth of your career. Treat it as a priority.

2 Create *aspiration* and *alignment* in your team. Find ways to *accelerate* change by engaging people at every level. An *agile* approach to change can create a "spiral of value" through which you constantly fight entropy by unlocking human energy.

3 Handle dilemmas by adopting a "both-and" mind-set, not an "either-or" mind-set. Make the tough choices must to fulfill a shared purpose, not just to meet your financial goals or metrics. Grab the bull by the horns rather than be impaled on the "horns of a dilemma."

Be like the fire, and wish for the wind.

—Nassim Nicholas Taleb

SECTION 3

GROWING CHANGE AGILITY

In this section, we aim to help you apply some of the ideas we've shared to grow your own leadership effectiveness and your team's performance to contribute to the development of a high-performance organization. There are many existing models and tools in this area; our intent is not to compete with these or seek to replace other models. Rather, we simply present our point of view on how change leadership in a VUCA world informs everything leaders need to do for their own development and for the wider organization.

A change-agile mind-set and practices are applicable at all levels and in several different contexts to support transformational change and also personal development. Making the shift toward change agility is itself a path that is unlikely to be simple or linear but complex and iterative.

Three Steps toward Winning with Change Agility: Me, My Team, and My Business

Me, My Team, My Business

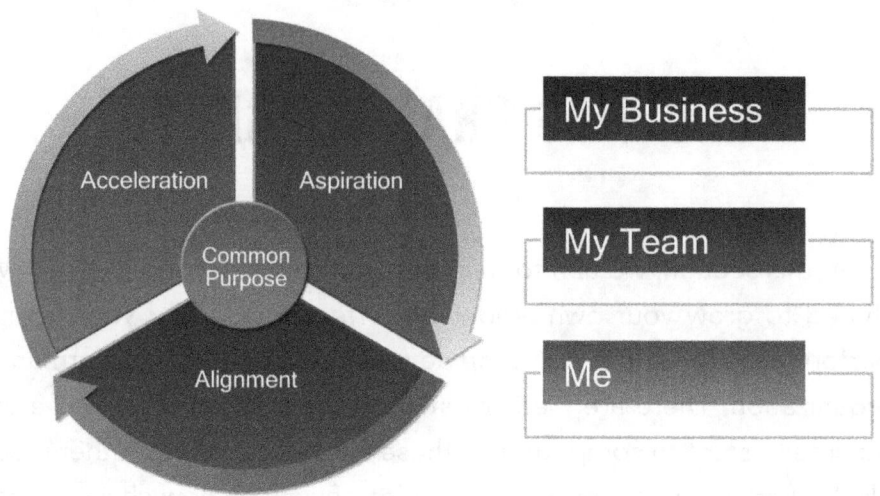

The starting point for growth in change agility is clarity on the core purpose of the organization and what it means to you, to your team, and to your peers across the business.

Purpose, in our experience, transcends both strategy and plans for the future. Purpose reflects the identity of the organization; it is a spiritual source of collective energy. Without this sense of identity, not only do individuals feel that something is missing, but the organization also fails to find its "true north" in the long run. That is why we think about the development of change agility as a process that begins with purpose. The primary challenge of change leadership in a VUCA world is to enable change with common purpose. Purpose has to permeate every layer in an organization—from the individual to the team and to the wider business. These are the three interconnected layers that need to be addressed.

Our model for change places the individual leader at the foundation of change and at the root of a winning culture, as per the diagram below.

Change Agility - Me, My Team, My Business

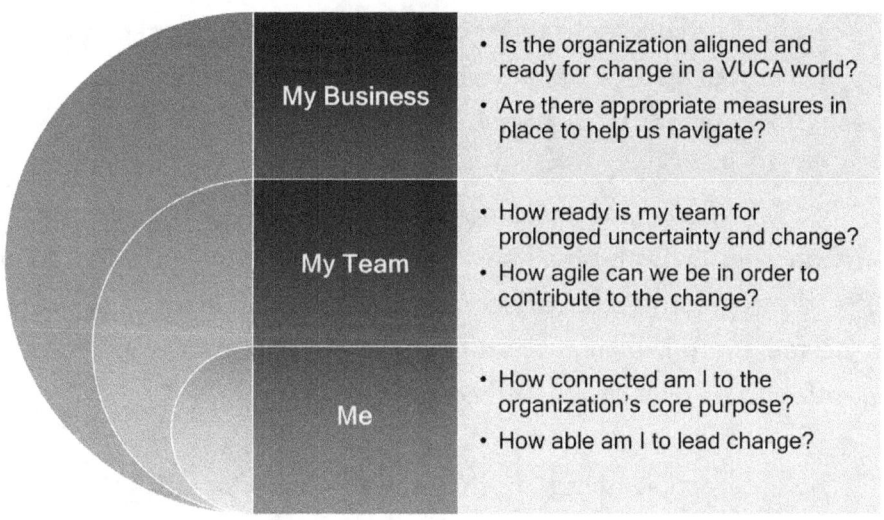

The leadership team is then the next building block for successful change. With enough effort, the whole business unit or organization can then be harnessed. Alignment of the three entities "me," "my team," and "my business" helps focus oneself, the leadership team, and the whole organization around the need for change agility.

Applying Agility: The Rise of Netflix and the Demise of Blockbuster Video

The movie-on-demand provider Netflix, in contrast to Blockbuster Video, shifted its business model successfully, showing change agility in action. Netflix was built on single-rental DVDs by mail in the '90s, copying the Blockbuster movie rental model but deploying it via the Internet. Netflix then switched to a monthly subscription model that was hugely successful. The success of this model combined with Blockbuster's own lack of agility after a period of market dominance resulted in Blockbuster's bankruptcy.

Today, Netflix has become known primarily for streaming video; its DVDs-by-mail service is actually dying out. Netflix even transformed its video streaming, its dominant business, to feel more like an alternative cable network on the Internet, offering its own shows and content.

The interesting thing in this sector is its significant convergence. Mobile service providers around the world, like Starhub and Singtel in Singapore, are creating revenue from streamed content on mobile devices. Even newspapers are now e-businesses. Across the TMT sector, companies need to execute strategy at the speed of change, to rethink their strategies to stay ahead, and to forge the right partnerships. Without agile leadership and change-ready organizations, all this is impossible.

Netflix now competes with major media distributors. A key decision to split out the legacy mail-order business from streaming and run it separately, using very agile technology and flexible ways of working created speed in a very dynamic, rapidly transforming sector.

Winning with Change Agility through Personal Leadership

Me, My Team, My Business

My Business

My Team

Me

Agility begins with leaders and the role they play in enabling high performance. The first questions to ask focus on the self and the extent to which one can lead change with the mind-set and skill of a change-agile leader. We place the individual leader at the heart of organization development and change and at the heart of a winning culture. Leadership in agile organizations is actually a collective responsibility with individually defined and mutually reinforcing accountabilities. Agility is not created purely hierarchically but in context. If a situation requires leadership from a senior executive's personal assistant, the personal assistant may need to be an agent of change. The list below outlines questions to ask yourself to assess how well equipped you are to lead change.

Quick Self-Assessment of My Change Agility

Change Agility for Me: Am I truly committed to the cause of winning for the greater good of the organization? To its core purpose?	Y/N
Aspiration: Are my personal aspirations connected to the cause?	
Am I purposeful enough in my choices and behaviors?	
Do I integrate different perspectives to manage complex issues sufficiently, even those I initially disagree with or that feel like opposites?	

Am I adequately inclusive as a leader and genuinely appreciative of diversity?	
Alignment: Am I clear and aligned to the right priorities at an emotional level, or do I feel that something is missing for me?	
Do I constantly seek to help others align around the need for change?	
Am I a strong enough champion for different kinds of creativity in how issues are addressed?	
Am I versatile enough in my style to handle ambiguity?	
Acceleration: Do I take action with speed, tenacity, courage, and commitment?	
Do I respond appropriately, decisively, and sensitively enough to the needs of my team, to the environment, and to my stakeholders?	
Do I adapt sufficiently to both short- and long-term priorities and changes in plans when needed?	
Do I show the right level of mental toughness in the face of big tests of my own commitment or courage?	

You can see in the description of change agility as it applies to your personal leadership that a fundamental question to ask from the outset relates to your own commitment to the greater good of the organization. This is important, because you will only show up as a change-agile leader if you can relate to the needs of the wider business, not just to your own priorities. It is then important to assess how connected your own aspirations are to the aspirations you believe the organization has for the future. It is helpful for you to consider your own aspirations in light of what is actually possible within the organization. This then helps you generate greater alignment of your priorities and emotional sense of engagement with the organization.

The final area of consideration for you as a leader relates to your capacity to take action with sufficient courage when necessary (based on the best information you can obtain). The last area requires a great deal of resilience in uncertain times. You can demonstrate resilience if you also look after your health and your personal well-being.

If we relate this approach to your own personal growth back to the four sources of energy we outlined in Part 1 (we present the diagram again for your convenience), then your strategies for development in each area might adopt some of the principles below.

Change Agility in is an on-going, informed and holistic response to uncertainty

Agility operates in the rational, emotional, behavioural and spiritual domains of human performance.

Harnessing all of these types of energy simultaneously can improve performance during times of change or uncertainty.

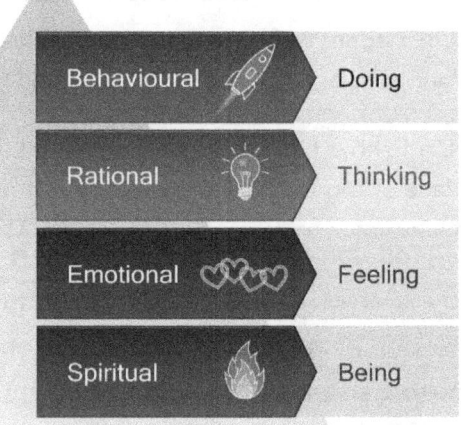

Rational Agility: Three Tips to Maximize Your Mental Alertness When and Where it Counts in an Uncertain World

Harness rational energy to help you make decisions in VUCA conditions and to make sense of all the information that bombards you. When faced with a difficult decision or piece of analytical thinking, create time and space to absorb all the information away from the office—somewhere quiet and peaceful where you can really focus your mind. Modern office environments do not always lend themselves to effective concentration, though they may encourage speed and volume of information. Create regular thinking and reflection time in your calendar to work through specific problems, and protect it.

Try not to overuse or depend too much on rational energy to the detriment of the other types. We find that corporate leaders, as they go through the ranks of large organizations, are encouraged to be overly analytical or data-rational in their style, and this can have negative side effects at times. People are not robots, and organizations are not machines. No matter how much data you gather and analyze, there will still be unknowns and uncertainty when facing strategic change in business. One must learn to work with available data and reasonable evidence, applying good executive judgment in the face of unknowns versus traditional rational decision making.

Give your mind a rest sometimes! Take breaks to recharge. Try not to overcomplicate or overanalyze complex challenges. Your instincts may well point you in the right direction when the road ahead seems less than clear cut. Mental clarity sometimes occurs when we least expect it if we just take some time to turn off and restart the mental operating system.

Emotional Agility: Three Tips to Maximize the Effectiveness of Your Emotional Responses to Change

Emotions are a source of power for motivating and driving our performance. Our emotions are like the horse, and our mind is the rider...one steers and guides the response of the other to unlock its power. Be aware of your emotions. Learn to manage and regulate them, and you will unlock the power of emotion in the way you lead. If you have a bad temper, for example, the key to better self-regulation is to learn to stop before you react. Positive thoughts that we consciously rehearse mentally help us experience more positive emotions, which in turn support better performance and the ability to cope better with change in a VUCA world.

One really helpful way to manage your emotional energy is to learn to take your time more often. In a VUCA world, we are rushed, overly busy, and often operating well outside our natural comfort zones. Some pressure and stress is healthy; it pushes our performance. However, unrelenting pressure (and, in particular, emotional stress) can be psychologically and physically damaging to your health in the longer term. Take your time whenever possible to reflect on your impulses and your feelings. Don't just react to these impulses in uncertain times. Pause and reflect before making critical decisions if you are able to. Slow down to speed up.

If you haven't already discovered mindfulness, then now is the time. Mindfulness is a discipline and a practice that helps you take more control of yourself and your emotions. Its essence is that you live your life in the present moment, paying attention to what is happening rather than wallowing in turbulent thoughts or emotions, especially those that are negative. Mindfulness helps you tune in properly to every aspect of what is really going on around you so that you have a fuller picture with which to form your conclusions.

Behavioral Agility: Three Tips to Maximize Your Ability to Be at the Top of Your Game During Times of Change

This is truly the age of the executive athlete. Modern business life for some requires endless travel, long office hours sitting at a desk, all-day meetings in air-conditioned meeting rooms (sometimes with no natural light), lots of rich foods in hotels and restaurants, high alcohol consumption, and various other ways to rapidly destroy one's well-being. The key to harnessing the energy to get things done is to remain physically active, taking sufficient exercise and managing your nutrition.

If you are not doing this, then one of the very first things you should do after reading this guide is to get a health assessment. Talk to a professional about practical ways in which you can improve your health with the right exercise and better nutrition so that you feel you have more energy for the challenges in your work and life. There is a form of exercise out there to suit everyone—from cycling to yoga to simple walking or stretching routines.

One CEO we have worked with puts weekly outdoor running slots into his weekly calendar no matter what country or time zone he happens to be in. This is a nonnegotiable time block for him. He does not cancel this running time for other urgent business matters. He has put staying healthy and resilient at the top of his list of success factors for his role as CEO. Even a small amount of regular physical activity is better than no activity. Make decent exercise part of your life.

One thing we just can't emphasize enough is the need to prioritize. This is challenging for many, we know. The demands on executives in today's world are at times insane. But the only person who will look after you in the end is you, especially in a business context. More likely than not, your employer will simply keep heaping challenges on you until you start to prioritize. Learning to manage the demands on your time, your priorities, and your personal well-being is critical to your agility in a permanently connected world. Cut out the pointless meetings, the unnecessary e-mails, and any after-work socializing that adds little real value to your business or career. Make time for personal relationships outside of your immediate work with people you trust. Take time also to be there for someone else in a completely nonbusiness-related sense, though, so that you retain a little perspective.

Try to reduce the number of meetings you attend. We find that some organizations have a meeting disease! Along with the e-mail disease, this can be a serious productivity drain. For every problem, the solution is to create a task force that simply meets every week, either on a call or face-to-face (or a mixture across different locations). Regular meetings are not always the most effective way to address issues or to collaborate around a shared priority.

Try to be more ruthless with the meetings, especially the regular standing meetings or committees that you initiate and accept. This will help you focus your action on the few things that will really help you, your team, and your organization to win. One large government organization's permanent secretary in the United Kingdom announced a "bonfire of committees" to the delight of all the civil servants who had spent endless hours stuck in a rut of all-day meetings and self-referential task forces.

Spiritual Agility: Three Tips to Connect Who You Really Want to Be With What You Do As a Leader

Research indicates that successful, enduring executives are those who have a connection with or sense of purpose beyond themselves and their career. They feel connected to the larger whole of life, which puts the day-to-day challenges and setbacks in their own career during times of change or uncertainty into context. These sorts of leaders also imbue this spirit into their teams, which also helps employees put things into perspective when times are tough.

Meaningful work can be done in a variety of ways. Spiritual agility helps you and those you lead work through complexity together. A sense of spirit does not require you to be religious or to spend weekends at mindfulness or yoga retreats, if that is not your sort of thing. One of the keys to harnessing your innermost resources, though, is finding a cause that matters to you or a mission that resonates with you. You don't have to "save the world" with your cause. Not all of us are driven to that. But as you reflect on this, some passion or interest that you can relate to your working life may come up. With it, you could unlock a reservoir of motivation and resilience you may have been missing.

An IT executive might quite simply be passionate about technology and its role in people's lives. Linking his or her role to this deeper instinct to make the world a better place through the application of technology might be a way to unlock deeper sources of motivation. Be clear on your professional purpose even when things appear to be uncertain around you, or when others might appear to work purely for job security or financial reward. Your sense of purpose will help you be clearer on your own personal value proposition and real mission.

In a VUCA world, it is possible that self-discovery is less important than self-creation or constant self-recreation. In today's business world, you are expected to be the architect of your own career and the owner of your own development, so you need deep clarity on the direction this needs to take. Taking the time away from the business of the office or your work location just to stop and think about your own development will help you find the personal resources you need to lead others through uncertain times. Try to create space for reflection and for personal growth.

Help others work through change. Offer them your support and your guidance. As you offer this support to others on their journeys, you will feel greater inner clarity on how you should navigate. Your instincts will take over. The key to unlocking spiritual energy is to be interested in the success of others. Change agility begins with this focus on the greater good.

How Change Agility Supports High
Performance in the Hospitality Sector

The hospitality sector is a rapidly evolving and globally highly interconnected web of brands, ownership, and operating structures. It is a sector where VUCA forces can play a very significant role at any level, and competition is fierce. If you happen to be the general manager of a five-star luxury resort with properties in Asia that are sometimes vulnerable to tsunamis or in parts of the Middle East prone to political instability and you've experienced periods of volatility, then you will know exactly what we are talking about.

Political conflicts and civil unrest can play a huge role in determining the success or failure of service-based companies with assets in these parts of the world. Leading hospitality groups invest in organizational capabilities, particularly in grooming the right people to lead hotel operations. One of the key capabilities that determine the success of an operational leader in hospitality is the ability to lead and manage change. The changes required in this industry are constant and relentless. Operational leaders at all levels must implement new policies, brand strategies, and changes to hotel processes and tools constantly. This kind of day-to-day operational change is then coupled with much deeper change associated with strategic initiatives that can be global or regional. Operational leaders must execute these initiatives, deciding how best to implement corporate initiatives locally.

Change agility in hospitality is needed at all levels, from global HQs to hotel operations. Global hospitality groups with multiple brands can use an agile, "asset-light" strategy to support their agility, scalability, and profitable growth as they work closely with hotel owners around the world. They also need to create equally agile organizations and leaders.

Customer Service Leadership

It is all too easy to become obsessed with operational results to the detriment of the well-being of people in your team in any frontline service environment. Managers are aware that running a good call center is all about motivating people even when the going is tough or when there is change in the air— which is generally constant in these operations.

For great customer satisfaction, managers must spend personal energy to build the capacity of their teams to work in a VUCA environment. Leaders in any fast-moving service sector (like hospitality, retail, food and beverage, or entertainment) aim to create unique experiences for their customers or guests that reflect their brands. Global brands like Starbucks take a great deal of trouble to help frontline staff serve customers in a way that reflects the brand. This is done at every stage in the customer's journey.

Starbucks, in fact, has not relied on television advertising since its inception but on its customer experience to create loyalty. This is all made possible by Starbucks's evident ability to implement changes in its worldwide network of outlets and to continuously improve experience. The Starbucks experience and format has undergone significant, ongoing innovation and transformation from the beginning.

Customer service and frontline sales teams of all sorts—global call center operations teams, multicountry IT helpdesks, hotel room bookings and sales teams, banking operations and product teams—need to have very agile ways of working to be able to deal quickly with change. The ability to implement change in these frontline environments almost effortlessly is a prerequisite to creating fantastic, both locally relevant and globally harmonized customer experiences.

Building Winning Teams with Change Agility

Me, My Team, My Business

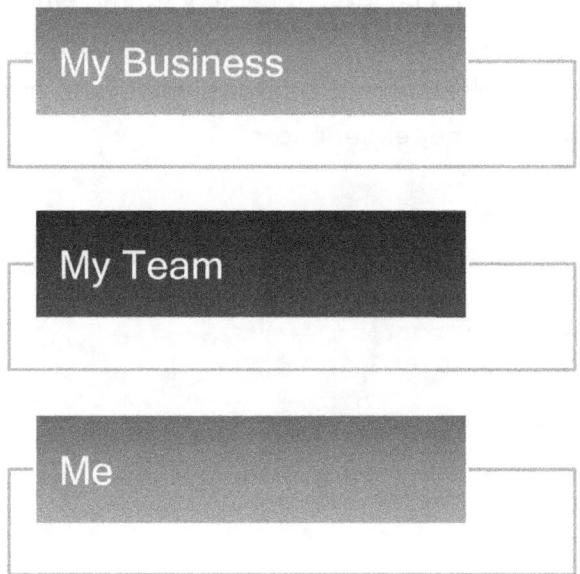

There are many very good frameworks and models for the development of high-performance teams. Research on high-agility Fortune 500 companies reveals a consistent factor in senior management teams for all highly agile firms: they do not allow decisions to be dominated by one or two individuals. The right executives with the right experience are always able to step up and manage the challenge facing the organization. These senior team members are self-aware enough to know when it is time to lead and when it is time to follow. They understand that each member brings a complementary skillset to the team and how to leverage the diversity of skills across the team.

Winning teams at the senior level exhibit agile leadership behaviors. Our approach to the growth of teams is to harness different kinds of energy and to connect team development directly with the growth of leaders and organizations. We find that all too often, different activities are not properly connected. This can create strange dislocations for people. What is the use, really, in investing heavily in building a great team, for example, if the leader's own behavior is completely misaligned or if the wider organization reinforces completely dysfunctional behavior? Our perspective is naturally a holistic view of the whole system in which people work. Healthy teams function at their best in healthy organizations.

Self-Assessment of Your Team

Change Agility for My Team: Does my team have a clear sense of the organization's core purpose, and is it shared right across the team?	Y/N
Aspiration: Do we as team have a shared aspiration?	
Do we purposefully drive toward this aspiration? How connected is the aspiration with the wider organization's purpose?	
Do we integrate different perspectives across the team?	
Are we inclusive and appreciative of people and views that challenge our own paradigms or views of the world?	

Alignment: Are we emotionally aligned to a joint set of priorities that will help the whole team move forward?	
Do team members feel ready to enable change together?	
Does the team have creative ways to address complex issues?	
Do we have the versatility to help the organization win?	
Acceleration: Are we as a team able to take action with speed, courage, and commitment?	
Are we responsive to the demands placed upon us, no matter how challenging or difficult they may seem?	
Do we adapt priorities when needed?	
Do people in the team have the mental toughness for the road ahead?	

Taking such a holistic view helps us see that a team wins by design. In constructing a change-agile team, we use every source of energy in the team to help the organization win. We unleash the problem-solving power of the team, the emotional drive and passion, the can-do action orientation, and the deeper sense of common purpose. All of this contributes to a feeling that the team is winning and that it is getting the desired results.

Shared purpose is, in our experience, the single most important factor in driving team performance. It is surprising how many teams we work with that do not have a sense of clarity around a common purpose (or even just a goal) that is connected to the purpose in the organization. In essence, change agility requires teams to feel that a deeper purpose exists for their work together as part of an enterprise. This then supports all of the other success factors that enable the team to be truly high performing.

Individual and collective aspiration to stretch outside personal and team boundaries is an essential feature of a change-agile team. Each individual team member must demonstrate genuine aspiration and go the extra mile for the team, constantly pushing the boundaries of his or her own capabilities. A team also needs to be sufficiently emotionally engaged and aligned around a joint set of priorities. People in the team need to be able to express their feelings openly and constructively without judgment by other team members. Members of the team who hold different perspectives should be able to work together to reconcile dilemmas and manage complex problems.

The final success factor for a team is then the ability to accelerate— to take action with conviction, working as one. Agile teams can respond to unforeseen circumstances without being derailed and can adapt to new priorities. Mental toughness is visible across the team so that when difficult challenges come up, the team has the personal and team resources not just to cope, but to win. Winning teams therefore connect the head, heart, hands, and spirit to make extraordinary things happen. Teams that are able to adapt to and benefit from change are vital building blocks for organizations that do the same. It is essential for organizations that aspire to be agile to invest in greater agility, not just in individual leaders but also in teams.

Change-agile teams are winning teams. They connect the doing, thinking, feeling, and being aspects of their work to operate in a VUCA world. Harnessing rational, emotional, behavioral, and spiritual energy simultaneously has far greater performance dividends than does developing any single aspect of the team's performance. We hear consultants of various kinds talk incessantly about the importance of "mind-set" and "behavior" in team effectiveness. What we aren't sure of is how much this captures sufficiently the emotional undercurrents and the deeper issues of identity within a team.

Rational Agility: Three Tips to Maximize Your Team's Ability to Deal with Complex Issues

Harness rational energy in your team to make the best possible decisions in VUCA conditions and to make sense of all the information that bombards you as a team. When faced with a difficult decision or piece of analytical thinking, create time and space for the whole team to absorb all the information together. Encourage debate and discussion of different interpretations of data rather than "groupthink." Appoint someone in the team to disagree with your most important and high-risk decisions to help you improve the quality of decisions.

Don't allow the team to overuse or depend too much on this source of energy to the detriment of other energies. Teams that are overly analytical or data-rational in their style can ignore the experience in the team or, indeed, in other parts of the organization. They can become isolated and absorbed in the problem-solving process instead of reaching out to other departments for support and help.

Give your team a rest sometimes from the challenges of dealing with complex issues. Create opportunities for easier, quick wins. Stop the team from overcomplicating things or overanalyzing complex issues. People's instincts may well point them in the right direction given a chance to just take a step back from the problem at hand.

Emotional Agility: Three Tips to Build a Positive and Healthy Team Climate

Emotions should not be swept under the carpet—they are a source of power to motivate and drive team performance. Be aware of the feelings within the team to unlock the power of emotion. The key to a better team climate is to be optimistic yourself and then encourage the whole team to feel the same. Optimism in a team can support better performance and the ability to cope better with change in a VUCA world.

One really helpful way to manage your team's emotional energy is to encourage people to take their time on the tasks that count. In a VUCA world, people in your team can feel very pressured at times to move fast. Some pressure and stress is healthy; it pushes the team's performance. However, unrelenting pressure (and, in particular, emotional stress) can be psychologically and physically damaging to the team and result in burnout. Allow people to take their time rather than simply demand more and more pace from them. In the long run, a team with a level of stress that is sustainable will be more likely to win.

It's not necessarily true at all that agility is all about speed, all of the time. It's about a burst of pace when it counts and concurrently being able to control the pace for best results.

The practice of mindfulness can be used as much by a team as it can by you as a leader. Mindfulness is a discipline and a practice that helps people in a team be more aware of their own emotions and those of others around them. Encourage team members to stay in the present and to pay attention to what is happening now rather than spend time dwelling on past events or things they cannot anticipate. Ask team members to concentrate on the present day's challenges. Staying in the present helps the team avoid anxiety about an uncertain future. High levels of anticipatory anxiety create stress and distraction from what can be done in the here and now.

Behavioral Agility: Three Tips to Maximize Your Team's Ability to Get Things Done in Uncertain Times

Expect your team members to look after themselves and their well-being in every sense. Don't judge those who do not conform to a long-hours culture if it is the norm in your organization. Long hours and the extension of work (or work-related travel) into every spare nook and cranny of life is a modern corporate affliction. If you feel that anything you are doing as a leader (or, indeed, what other team members are doing) is impacting the health of people negatively, then take a step back to look at how you can create a more sustainable, healthier way of working.

Providing people in the team with the time to recover and to access health facilities is one way simply to encourage people to take care of themselves. You also show your care for them as a leader. We have seen countless examples of places where people feel they need to be the last one out of the office (or should not leave until the boss has left). What really matters in today's complex organizations is not how long we are in the office but our contributions to the organization's goals and core mission.

It is vital to the energy level in your team, especially in challenging times of change, for people to get sufficient rest and to detach themselves regularly. Be more curious about the things that matter to your team members regarding their personal health and well-being. They are likely to have passions outside work—even simple things like time with their children, if they have families. Sensitivity toward the needs people have outside the office environment is important in a leader with change skills. It is hard to implement change in burned-out teams.

As a leader, you can help people to prioritize and manage their time effectively. If you notice that the team or any of its members are burning out, find out what is creating the unsustainable pressure for them. Take an interest in this rather than turn a blind eye. Cut out all the things in the team's schedule that you think might be creating rework or unnecessary effort so they can focus on the really important things. Focus is good for performance.

Remember, the question to ask yourself every day in a team about any new project you are initiating is, "Will it make the boat go faster?" Having spent considerable time within organizations, not just advising, it is clear to us that corporate life is full of activity that we do simply because of the pressure to appear busy. Teams can unconsciously create busywork for various reasons—often when there is some kind of insecurity or crisis of identity in the work group. Busywork is the enemy of change agility and purposiveness in a team.

Courage is one of the keys to performance in volatile situations. As a leader of change, you need to show that you have the personal courage to make choices and to take action when it counts, rather than avoid accountability. If you demonstrate your ability to be accountable for your actions, your team will do the same. In this area, you must lead by example. Teams take the lead from the team leader when it comes to their overall propensity for risk. Without any risk propensity, it is unlikely that a team will learn or evolve.

A simple way to demonstrate risk propensity in a corporate environment is occasionally to adopt the "better to seek forgiveness than permission" principle when making decisions that might usually require upward escalation. Show that you are able to work outside the organization's boundaries of control every now and then, and people will see that it is OK to exercise their own judgment.

Spiritual Agility: Three Tips to Maximize Your Team's Sense of Purpose and Mission

Try your best to harness the passion or interests within your team and show how they connect to your common purpose. Appeal to these personal interests and connect with them on a personal level, not just a task level. Be clear and open with your team on your professional purpose and help members create clarity for themselves around what matters most to each of them in their professional lives. Part of your role as a leader is to be an inner compass or, indeed, an anchor for others, especially during tough times. Some of this comes through your own professionalism.

A team with strong identity tends to behave professionally regardless of the situation. For example, a good human resources team supporting a business unit through change while also being part of a global HR transformation exercise should be able to rely on a strong sense of professional identity and execute on both agendas.

Help people in the team be their best selves through coaching. Coaching is about drawing out solutions from people, taking them somewhere they wouldn't go on their own. A leader needs to coach people at several points during change. Spend time with each of the people in your team, coaching them on performance, handling underperformance, and encouraging them to reflect on their aspirations for their own careers and futures. Show the team in your coaching conversations that you represent a cause that is bigger than any of you. This is a way to tap deeper resources in the whole team as you lead them through change.

Ask the team members to offer each other plenty of personal support and challenge. As they do, they will start to feel greater inner clarity for themselves. Help them unlock their own instincts for the purpose of problem solving and decision making—avoid too much spoon-feeding. The key to unlocking spiritual energy in the team is for members to take an interest in each other's success, not just their own. Change agility begins with this focus on a shared purpose that goes beyond the individual. Team members must learn through this process that no one is bigger than the team.

A point to emphasize here is that as a leader, you must ensure that you are having the right conversations at the right times. When necessary, address any underperformance directly and without hesitation.

The emotional agility and the courage to have these sorts of conversations with team members is important to any difficult change process. Courageous conversations take place in relation to every aspect of the model we have described: in mental, emotional, behavioral, and personal or spiritual domains of our working lives. Being able to talk about our ideas, feelings, choices and innermost drivers is important for relationships to go beyond the superficial. A courageous conversation connnects what you say with how you feel and what you would like see happen in light of certain facts. It also allows others to say what they think, what they feel, and what they would like to see happen. Mature and adult dialogue is the key to managing performance issues before they become serious setbacks to change.

Public Service Transformation Requires Change Agility

During the financial crisis of 2008, a slowdown in the UK private sector was accompanied by a major reduction in UK government spending after a 2010 election and a change in political leadership. The impetus for this was rapidly escalating public debt that the government determined had become uncontrolled.

One of the most important and high-profile areas for policy reform the new Coalition government embarked upon was transformation of the UK welfare sector, which under the previous government had grown substantially. This required a fundamental rethink of policy, systems, organization structure, delivery model, and every other aspect of how British citizens receiving different types of welfare services, from income support to pensions, were served by government.

The government initiated a policy initiative named "Universal Credit," which was a simplified benefit system with new rules and procedures using a new technology platform. Government transformation initiatives, especially those that have involved the delivery of large-scale IT systems, have often been subject to criticism for being slow, expensive, and misaligned to the needs of their key stakeholders. Prior attempts to overhaul the National Health Service's IT in the United Kingdom met huge resistance from frontline clinical professionals.

The overhauled UK welfare system will take years to implement. Leaders have stated the importance of building the capacity for change within the civil service to support these new systems, and an "agile software development" approach was adopted. The adoption of change-agile ways of thinking and working is making a difference in UK public service to ensure successful delivery of policy in a complex setting.

Agile India: Applying Change Agility to Drive Growth

India's IT sector, which has grown up in the last two decades, is one of the great economic miracles to occur in the developing world. Change agility is a driver for growth, with companies like Infosys, Wipro, Tata Consulting Services, and Cognizant leading the charge into India's technology-enabled future. These companies have rapidly proven themselves to be globally competitive.

If we look at the growth of this sector from a client's point of view, although one of the key drivers to offshore IT services to India is to cut costs, this is far from the only benefit to be derived for companies that outsource. Outsourcing is a great way to gain organizational flexibility quickly if it is managed well. Research in this area has found that companies who outsource increase organizational agility and state that this is one of the top drivers guiding their sourcing decisions.

Research also shows that successful offshoring efforts to India have led to greater flexibility and change capability. With offshore and outsourced capabilities in technology and other business functions, corporations can redesign processes, enhance efficiencies, improve service quality, and enable more effective access to new markets and sources of innovation.

Accenture has featured in another one of our examples. In 2004, Accenture had around eighty thousand employees worldwide and only a relatively small fraction of these people were in India. In ten years, the headcount grew to 275,000 people worldwide and eighty thousand in India. Accenture in India has embraced change ever since its formation. Accenture's outsourcing business is an exemplar of change agility and has been instrumental in transforming the firm into an outsourcing giant.

Building Winning Organizations with Change Agility

Me, My Team, My Business

Everyone in an organization, no matter what role or level in the hierarchy, can and should contribute to the development of a winning organization—one that demonstrates all of the change-agile attributes needed in a VUCA world. Change agility at the enterprise level also harnesses every kind of human energy—mental, emotional, physical, and spiritual or personal—to manage complexity and drive transformation.

There are many features of a change-agile organization that may help it win. In organization design or architecture terms, change agility touches on every aspect of a business including strategy, structure, quality of human capital, incentives, tools, technologies, processes, partnerships, locations, and geographic footprint. Our approach to the development of change agility requires leaders to identify business-critical challenges that impact the overall effectiveness of the whole organization so that leaders can address these together, working as one.

We have already shared a model for cultural change agility. This model is relevant to the development of change capability at an organizational level. We do not believe there is a one-size-fits-all solution to the design of an organization, and our intent is not to provide a manual on organization design. However, in each of these seven areas, your organization would benefit from showing the ability to reconcile dilemmas or resolve tensions that get in the way of agile performance.

Seven Cultural Orientations which give rise
to cultural dilemmas

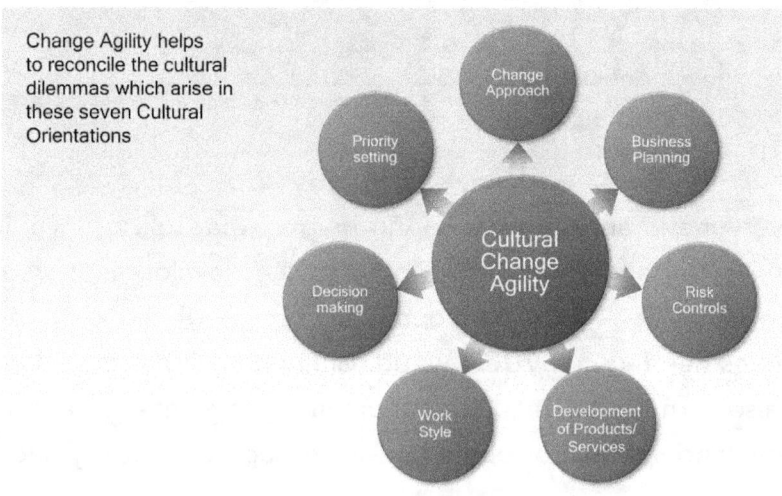

What we also find is that change agility is particularly visible and impactful during what we call "cultural moments of truth." These are the defining moments when people need to be at their very best and where the design of the organization has the highest business impact.

Moments of truth exist in every organization. The idea of them was originally developed in relation to customer experience by experts in branding and customer service. Several services-based organizations in sectors such as hospitality, retail, and entertainment (perhaps most famously Disney) have applied this concept to help transform customer or client experience during their own moments of truth. Companies like Virgin and Disney pioneered the use of moments of truth to create branded customer experiences.

Figuring out what your own moments of truth are from an internal cultural perspective, linking these to what your customers or stakeholders deem to be important, and then finding ways to differentiate your business at moments of truth is a focused approach to organizational design and development. BSkyB in the United Kingdom (the largest pay-TV broadcaster there and in Ireland, with ten million subscribers) has used this methodology to successfully shape its internal culture and align it with the desired quality of customer experience.

The key success factors of change agility—the practices we associate with high performance during uncertain times—need to be particularly evident during your own internal moments of truth. Take time to reflect on what these are in your organization and define what you think "great" looks like in these moments. Then work toward it. This is a far more effective way to influence culture or behavior at scale than are internal poster campaigns or generic discussions about culture or values.

One implication of an emerging area of thought known as "complexity science" for how we can create more change-agile institutions is that we can have an impact on culture through specific moments in the value chain of a business that disproportionately affect its performance. This has some similarity to the "butterfly effect" in complexity theory in which small changes in a complex system can have a massive effect on the whole system. Complexity science has influenced our thinking about change a great deal. Our view is that it is practically impossible to create meaningful change in an entire global organization's culture directly or overnight through simply describing the desired culture. What is needed is focused attention to specific issues related to the critical challenges in the business that can impact the culture. This is an action-oriented approach rather than a purely mind-set-oriented approach.

We have seen little evidence that the traditional facilitation methods organizational coaches use to attempt to shift mind-set create the value or cultural impact that they purport to. Be wary of consultants and coaches who offer you any kind of oversimplified panacea for shifting the mind-sets of thousands of employees in a global enterprise. It isn't as simple as rolling out a series of workshops with a talented speaker or facilitator. All too often, that seems to be the method clients use to try to shift their cultures—and to little avail.

We have seen several large global organizations attempt to transform their businesses by sending teams of external trainers to their various locations to run very generic workshops with groups of managers and employees. Although helpful in some ways, having been involved in many such programs, it is clear to us that culture rarely changes in any visible or lasting way purely as a result of highly stage-managed performance coaching experiences.

Facilitated dialogue is important, and clearly there is a need for a base level of awareness and buy-in to the need for change across an enterprise. However, the content and focus of the dialogue is eventually the key to value creation. Generic conversations about the need for mind-set shifts, shared values, or leadership behavior do not alone help managers address complex organizational issues that get in the way of high-performance culture. Nothing can replace the kind of serious dialogue that occurs in working together across internal silos on-real world business problems, resolving the natural tensions in the organization, as a vehicle for personal development and deep change. We see real results when emphasis shifts from the generic to the specific and toward deliberate efforts related to the organization's cultural moments of truth.

There are four key steps for behavioral change to occur within cultural moments of truth:

1. Communicate about what needs to change in specific terms and through powerful, real-life stories.
2. Enroll leaders in the right kind of development to fill capability gaps.
3. Help sponsors and leaders act as strong role models for change with coaching if required.
4. Sustain behavioral change within moments of truth with the right operational tools, organization structures, processes and procedures, aligned incentives, support, enablement, and recognition.

The diagram below illustrates this process and how it helps to build a change-agile organization.

Transform behaviour during Cultural Moments of Truth - the defining moments where your organization needs to be the best it can be and where successful transformation is most critical

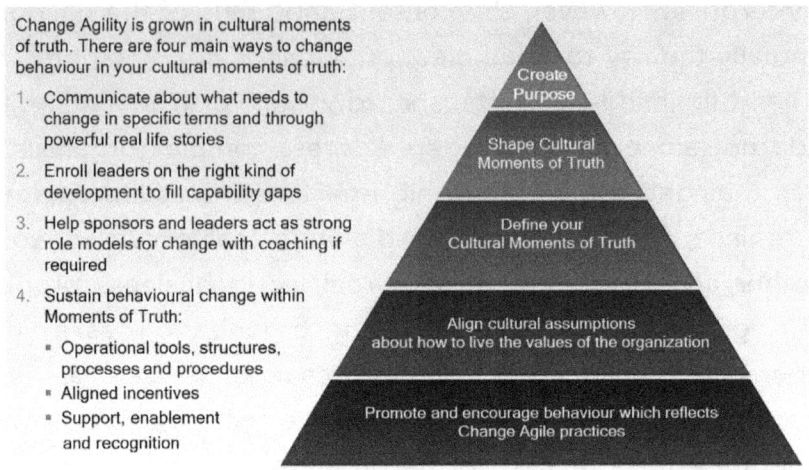

Change Agility is grown in cultural moments of truth. There are four main ways to change behaviour in your cultural moments of truth:

1. Communicate about what needs to change in specific terms and through powerful real life stories

2. Enroll leaders on the right kind of development to fill capability gaps

3. Help sponsors and leaders act as strong role models for change with coaching if required

4. Sustain behavioural change within Moments of Truth:
   - Operational tools, structures, processes and procedures
   - Aligned incentives
   - Support, enablement and recognition

Create Purpose

Shape Cultural Moments of Truth

Define your Cultural Moments of Truth

Align cultural assumptions about how to live the values of the organization

Promote and encourage behaviour which reflects Change Agile practices

What we feel is lacking in many attempts to go "from good to great," or to build a high-performance culture, is the connection to specific moments in the life of the organization where transformation really needs to be most evident and where it differentiates. It helps if the lens adopted to identify these moments is external (so that you are looking into the business from outside). A high-performance culture should ultimately serve an external group of stakeholders, especially its customers, whoever they may be, with exceptional agility. We know that customers' preferences and tastes change quickly, especially since competitors are always thinking of ways to entice them away from us. For example, in a retail outlet, or hotel, the arrival of a customer or a guest can be both a customer's moment of truth and a cultural moment of truth, in which the whole organization brings to bear its capabilities. This can be a critical point in time when the trust of a new customer is either created or undermined.

Assessment of Change Agility in Your Business, Department, Function, or Division

Change Agility for My Business: Given my understanding of our core purpose as an organization, does it have emotional significance and sufficient meaning for us?	Y/N
Aspiration: Does the (business, department, function, or division) have a shared aspiration?	
Are we purposeful as an organization?	
Do we integrate different perspectives?	
Are we inclusive and appreciative of diversity of thought?	
Alignment: Are we emotionally and practically aligned with a joint plan of action?	
Do we help people align around the kind of transformation that is needed?	
Do we encourage creativity in how we solve problems?	
Are we versatile enough to stay ahead of our competitors?	
Acceleration: Are we able to take action with speed, courage, and commitment?	

Are we responsive to the economic environment and to the market?	
Do we adapt our strategies and plans when needed?	
Are we resilient in the face of practical challenges and tests of our courage?	

The key success factors for change agility can be applied to a business, function, geographic unit, or other substructure within an organization as well as to the whole enterprise. The overarching purpose for people across the enterprise is the focal point. Everything grows from this shared purpose, around which there must be clarity.

The development of shared purpose is a major undertaking in its own right. It requires recognition of an institution's tradition and identity plus clarity on how its identity must evolve to create its future. Purpose creates a connection between the past, present, and future. It fosters leadership with an emphasis on positive legacy. The level of aspiration across different units, consistency in the level of collaborative behavior, and integration across silos are all critical to support core purpose. Alignment to shared priorities, constructive problem solving, and versatility to adopt outside-the box methods all help to create an emotionally engaged, positive cultural environment.

An organization also needs to be able to move fast and in a unified way to respond to competitive threats or to customer demands when necessary. This is especially important when leading transformational change. Change-agile organizations are winning organizations. They connect the doing, thinking, feeling, and being aspects of work to manage complexity and harness change. Winning organizations grow and tap human energy at all levels. Winning organizations harness the rational, emotional, behavioral, and spiritual domains of human performance. Harnessing all of these types of energy simultaneously can improve enterprise performance and help to manage long-term organization transformation.

Collective responsiveness, speed, and resilience are all components of the kind of culture that can support real benefits from change. Organizations that struggle with these things may never turn change rhetoric into reality. We can see the importance of mental, behavioral, emotional, and spiritual energy in organizations that adapt to external forces habitually—where people are aligned to the need for constant transformation. These properties enable organizations to find ways to benefit from uncertainty in external conditions.

Here are some tips to harness each source of organizational energy.

Rational Agility at the Enterprise Level: Three Tips to Harness Collective Creativity

Make planning, joint problem solving, and thinking about the business feel like fun. We find that so many companies create a real sense of dread in their senior leaders and other staff when it comes to strategy development, planning, and other important, mentally challenging activities. This work is serious, but it does not always have to be quite so intimidating or formal. The less formal it is, the more likely people will come up with new ways to think about the future of the organization, higher aspirations, and better, more creative solutions to complex dilemmas.

Monthly business-update or sales-forecast review meetings in a hierarchical sales or marketing function is a typical situation in which just lightening the atmosphere a little might help alleviate the stress people experience at them. Fear of reprisal by superiors may stop people from being open and honest about the true state of the business in a public forum. Such certainly stops executives from offering their most creative solutions to problems.

Review how you build strategy. Bring external ideas or data into your planning processes that feel countercultural, even a little unsettling for your executives. Being put outside our usual frames of reference can help us see things from interesting and different points of view. Executives in organizational silos are frequently trapped in their own mental models and cultural norms. Shaking things up a little with ideas from the outside world can be a useful antidote.

Spend more time planning for several short-term wins as you pursue your mission rather than building detailed, five-year strategies. Strategy development itself needs to be a much more agile, emergent discipline in a VUCA world than it has been.

Aspiration grows exponentially when we physically bring people together to think, debate, inquire, and learn from each other. In the globalized and virtual team environment many leaders now work within, it is challenging to create space for face-to-face workshops. However, in our experience, events designed to open up possibilities, to generate solutions in a team setting, are powerful ways to create stronger human connections while also creating value for the enterprise.

Emotional Agility across a Winning Organization: Three Tips to Make Better Use of Emotion during Change

It is really helpful first to understand how people are actually feeling in the organization. Clearly, engagement and surveys have served an important purpose in this regard. However, what these tools cannot replace is the process of talking to people directly and in a nonjudgmental way about their feelings. While feelings are not usually considered appropriate substance for corporate meetings, feelings are part of our lives at work. Understanding people's feelings across an organization through face-to-face focus groups, discussions, and Q&A sessions is essential.

Reframe resistance as concern and understand it through dialogue. (We discussed this in the last section.) At the organization level, much resistance actually arises as a result of people's concerns about the organization and the direction it is moving in. Their careers and possibly livelihoods are, after all, potentially at stake. Finding ways to clarify concerns also helps to stop them from escalating into more serious forms of resistance to change.

When talking to groups, leaders of change should be able to communicate and share their own emotions rather than just speak from prepared PowerPoint slides. Emotion is best conveyed and harnessed through personal stories, not formal content. Leaders who are able to share real-life stories that bring out their own experiences and insights help others feel that they are being led by human beings too. Leaders should speak to their own hopes and fears, showing that they do understand the challenges and emotional realities of change. If you occupy a formal leadership position, aim to share stories that reduce the psychological distance between you and those whose trust and confidence you seek. Storytelling is not an opportunity for self-aggrandizement. It is a means of building authentic connection and should be an indication of your true empathy for people who work with you.

Behavioral Agility in a Matrix Organization: Three Ways to Combine the Benefits of an Aircraft Carrier and a Fighter Jet

Organization design matters. Many modern organizations use various forms of "matrix" structure so that different reporting structures naturally overlap. Structuring a business for agility is critical to success. This means ensuring that where the structure needs to be tight (according to our "loose-tight" model), it is appropriately controlled, measured, and consistent. However, a structure also needs to allow sufficient room for movement, growth, and creativity where those are needed, so in these areas it should be "loose." For example, the role of corporate HQ may be to set the right standards for the corporate functions in local subsidiaries around the world. It should also allow the corporate offices in high-growth markets to decide how best to structure themselves for successful market penetration locally. Think about where your organization has to be tight and where it has to be loose by design to show maximum agility.

Corporate leaders and team members should be rotated into roles (not just *locations*) that require them to unlearn what they "know" and replace it with new ways of working. This is a helpful way to ensure that from a leadership perspective, people can flex their styles according to the needs of different environments and situations. Flexibility of response only accumulates when people are exposed to a variety of problems and business environments. We find that in organizations where people are left to build their careers within a single role for very long periods, there is a lower ability to adjust quickly to changing demands.

Location is a different and more complicated issue. There is intrinsic value in immersing people in different cultures, particularly in complex, global functions. However, this can be achieved without uprooting executives and forcing global mobility. The key to the globally dexterous behavior needed from international executives in a global matrix may be relocation that is not always physical. Creating behavioral agility may be more subtle than requiring stints at HQ, for example.

In fact, the key may be to change the location of the *critical roles*—to decentralize them and do away altogether with the concept of a dominant headquarters in a home country. Increasingly, we see examples of global roles being conducted in Western corporations from Asian locations such as Singapore or Hong Kong. This is good for agility and creates career opportunities in the organization outside its country of origin.

Reinforce agility with the right rewards and incentives at all levels, especially at senior ones. Create strong incentives for leaders to treat change as part of their roles in the form of appropriately designed bonus and profit-sharing schemes. Set up local recognition systems for regions to celebrate successful change. Reward and recognize change that is done well and that helps the organization move forward in tough times: this is a key enabler of agility.

All this goes hand in hand with a performance system that also creates real accountability for change at leadership levels. Leadership objectives and metrics need to be aligned to the transformational agenda of the business, not just its operational priorities. Recognition of adaptability without financial inducements can take many forms. The concept of recognition, for example with an awards programme, is used by agile organizations in different ways to create incentives for people to embrace change. Seek to put in place recognition for those who are adaptive, who set the tone for critical changes needed for your organization to remain competitive.

Spiritual Agility: Three Ways to Build Spirit while Driving Transformation

Building a real sense of spirit in a large, diverse organization is a tough outcome to achieve. However, without this, the organization and its leaders may sometimes seem to lack a pulse. Work can be a deeply fulfilling and empowering activity for all of us. Creating spirit in the workplace is done by relating what people do to a cause and then showing that the organization is serious about it through visible congruence.

If the cause is compassionate or service oriented, then you need to demonstrate that you embrace the underlying ethic in everything the organization does. If you say that you exist to "improve the lives of the world's consumers," then do that always and without too many exceptions—and start by improving the lives of the people in your own organization. If you are a health care company and say you want to make patients your priority, put the company's money where your mouth is. As a customer-centric financial services organization, show your concern for clients' needs visibly by rewarding and recognizing people who demonstrate it, not just those who tactically sell the most profitable products. If you are a human resources leader, then demonstrate your passionate care for people every day in the way the HR function supports people: put the "human" back into human resources.

Every time you compromise the spirit of your mission to create short-term wins or score personal career points, you risk undermining the spirit that fires up the company. This diminishes success in the long term because it creates a cynical culture and, inevitably, self-serving behavior.

Show that you personally have a sense of spirit that you bring to your work. One leader in a large investment firm we have worked with proclaimed to his management team in one of his off-site meetings, "I do have a pulse"—when his behavior provided no evidence of it whatsoever. In one large, town-hall type meeting, this leader announced a restructure that seriously affected the roles of individuals within his own direct leadership team, and he had failed even to share this detail with some of them ahead of the public announcement—at which they were present—let alone consult them or involve them in the design process. He showed no genuine compassion or care for the people he managed on a day-to-day basis, at times visibly losing his temper with junior and senior people in his department.

However, when recruiting capable people, or when in the presence of the CEO or the senior stakeholders he served, he was naturally, utterly charming and respectful. He was quite clearly motivated entirely to get results, to be seen to be a strong leader and to grow his own profile at any cost to his team. He surrounded himself with good people with excellent track records, who were regularly hired opportunistically without any sense of clarity about their roles or even whether the organization was actually right for them. However he kept losing key members of the department he was building within months of them joining. Suffice to say that his reputation outside the organization was not good and this also affected future recruitment efforts. Even though there are unfortunately many leaders we come across like this who can survive in organizations, even to thrive politically, their legacy is often tarnished and they leave a trail of misery behind them. This is no cause for pride and in the long run it does not get results.

Demonstrate that you care about your clients and your colleagues in meaningful ways. The more you do this as a leader, the more people around you will seek to serve the organization's purpose rather than to derive personal gain. If legacy matters to you and other leaders in your organization, then authenticity and congruence, even kindness, do all make a difference to your reputation.

Moral clarity is difficult to achieve in large organizations, yet it is also deeply important to their survival. By moral clarity, we mean the kind of ethical standards and even the human ideals that enable organizations to serve their stated purposes. Simply putting in place a code of conduct or writing down the corporate values is not enough. Just training people to be aware of the firm's values and standards is a step forward; however, it is also entirely inadequate.

In the end, leaders and managers across the organization need to know how to put values into action every day during cultural moments of truth. Having the personal and collective resources to reconcile complex ethical dilemmas, working often across several different cultural standards, is the heart of leadership in today's business world.

Our real concern is less the big corporate failures like Enron, whose CEO is jailed, but more the insidious impact of smaller but equally damaging, everyday, invisible ethical compromises in the trenches of organizations. The financial services sector has been particularly prone in recent history to ethical failures at all levels. More can and should be done to ensure that every aspect of your organizational culture and leadership is aligned to your stated purpose and values. This imperative creates particular issues in some newly liberalized, developing markets where business practices can be quite corrupt under an immature rule of law. Ethical choices must be made. It is the ultimate challenge of leadership in a VUCA world for executives to grow their businesses in challenging, uncertain markets, and to deal with difficult situations, while also living up to the values they espouse at a corporate level. Simply treating those you work with at all levels in a humanizing and empowering, ethical manner is a good start. We have witnessed many examples of executives doing the opposite. Every time someone is psychologically undermined in the workplace the moral fiber of the organization erodes just a little. We are not advocating that we should wrap people in emotional cotton wool. People do need to be resilient, to make their own choices about how they react to and tolerate a degree of human frailty, even in those who occupy leadership roles. However if behavior in the workplace is not tempered with a high level of dignity in all human interactions, our concern is that this actually can be a step towards lack of respect for broader social context as a whole and the commensurate moral ideals in a society. In certain industries enterprise agility rests upon the invisible coercion of employees from developing countries to adopt extremely demanding ways of working in order to achieve incredibly difficult feats. Construction, manufacturing and tourism booms in various parts of the Middle East and Asia provide ample evidence. Some aspects of today's economic transformation in developing countries are less illustrative of agility, as of the ease of human exploitation. The ethical and spiritual slope is slippery. Agility is only genuine if all those involved at every level can exercise greater personal choice, if employees are treated in a dignified, equitable way and not like a commodity. This is a definitive feature of spiritual agility at the enterprise level.

Important Note on Applying Change Agility: It Is Not a Silver Bullet

Our point of view on change agility as an organizational capability is not that it is a simple formula for excellence or longevity in the business world—if indeed excellence or longevity are the right aims for all modern organizations. Change agility represents a set of interconnected practices that are highly contextual and open to interpretation by leaders in all sorts of businesses.

Based on the research we have reviewed and our experience as psychologists specializing in change, the elements of change agility are increasingly necessary but not sufficient ingredients for success. There is ample evidence that companies who build their change capability are less likely to become victims of circumstance and more likely to turn potential crisis into opportunity.

In a study of the performance success factors and derailers of ninety Fortune 500 companies over an eleven-year period, it was clear that agility is promoted by certain consistent cultural norms such as shared purpose. In agile cultures, net income growth was exponentially higher than in nonagile cultures over that period. However, agility can also be undermined by cultural norms such as conflict avoidance. What is essential in the long term for any organization to develop change agility is to reinforce the cultural norms that promote it and to eliminate the agile-culture derailers.

The reality is that managing an adaptive, high-performance culture is a juggling act that requires constant attention and effort. Our perspective is that change agility simply creates a language and a model in which to anchor efforts that relate to adaptive culture. It seems fair to assume that only a few organizations can achieve and sustain a truly change-agile culture given the number of potential derailers inherent in organizational life. This point should serve as both a provocation and a reality check for leaders who believe that building a change-agile culture is anything other than deeply challenging (and is therefore a real competitive differentiator).

Many forces operate against you in this regard, including the human tendency to do what is expedient rather than right. The list of agile-culture derailers and agility-promoting cultural norms serves as a quick guide to the outcomes of the Fortune 500 study. You can see the strong overlap with our checklists and agility-promoting behaviors.

The table below identifies some cultural hallmarks of an agile organization. These cultural attributes require management and leadership attention to build the kind of winning organization many corporations would like to be. Our efforts with clients often revolve around building the agility-promoting cultural norms listed in the second table. In a sense, this is our own mission as organizational psychologists: to create healthy institutions in which these cultural traits *are* the norm. They map easily and well onto the success factors of change agility we articulated in Section 1.

Agile Culture Derailers
(R. Roi and S. Flatt, "Agile Cultures and ROI," 2005)

Promoted and Valued Cultural Norms	Is this a cultural norm in your organization? Yes or No/ Comments
Perfectionism People feel they must avoid making mistakes.	
Internal Competition People are rewarded for outperforming each other.	
Conflict Avoidance People tend to avoid conflict and work hard to keep relationships pleasant.	
Keeping Low Performers We put more effort into developing low performers than motivating and rewarding high performers.	

Agility-Promoting Cultural Norms

Promoted and Valued Cultural Norms	Is this a cultural norm in your organization? Yes or No/ Comments
Consistent Set of Guiding Values We apply a clear and consistent set of values to govern the way we do business.	
Risk Taking and Innovation Employees in our company are encouraged to take risks and apply innovative new ideas.	
Teamwork and Cross-Unit Collaboration Employees in our company are empowered to work across internal boundaries and collaborate with other departments.	
Organizational Learning Our company continually invests in improving the knowledge and skills of employees.	
Shared Purpose Employees have a clear sense of mission that gives them direction and purpose for their work.	

The Future of Work in Change-Agile Professional Services Organizations

Global professional services firms, especially consulting firms, are increasingly agile in the way they design offices, working tools, technologies, and teams for people to serve global clients.

Many consulting and services firms, such as Accenture or BT Group, have embraced agile ways of working to serve global clients across multiple locations seamlessly and flexibly. Virtual teams work in multiple time zones to provide expertise and support across a client's set of diverse business requirements.

Consulting firms are particularly good at creating new structures quickly through pools of flexibly deployed, skilled resources to implement client solutions. Marriott, for example, has publicized work with Accenture to outsource its global business services for hotels. Accenture has announced that the firm would adopt Marriott's business services function to support this while also using it as a platform for its strategic growth in the hospitality sector. This is a creative way to streamline corporate functions for global hospitality groups.

People at Accenture tend not to talk about work as a fixed place they go to but about the projects they do for clients. Outside of delivering client solutions, everything else in a professional services firm, including its structure, is more or less just fluff. Flexible use of hot desks, great knowledge management, telecommuting, virtual collaboration tools, roles that are skill based and not job based— all of these help Accenture move fast to create opportunities.

Being able to anticipate and then exploit trends to solve some of their clients' most difficult business problems is in Accenture's heritage and cultural DNA.

Effective Strategic Partnering Requires Change-Agile Leadership in IT

Infrastructure and IT developments regularly require partnering for major projects. This is also true in real estate, telecom, and power and energy projects. Joint ventures and strategic partnerships are classic scenarios that can create significant human challenges. Many of the usual change management disciplines come to the foreground in large partnering arrangements. But change agility is critical to successful and ambitious partnership.

It is important to be clear from the outset on the purpose of a partnership. It should help employees in each organization feel excited and passionate about its success. Leaders across all the participating organizations must have shared aspirations for the venture. Critically, they will need to work together across several different cultures. This is a common challenge in cross-border ventures and partnerships requiring many of the capabilities we have described in *Change Agility*, especially shared purpose and aspiration as well as deep alignment.

We have seen many very large technology partnering arrangements fail, including public-private partnerships, due to the
lack of clearly articulated, jointly held aspirations; poor alignment to joint working; and low ability to solve problems collaboratively. A high-profile program failure in public health care
transformation in the United Kingdom that was partly due to
serious infighting between members of a large IT consortium
illustrates the need for agility. Stronger collaboration efforts
are needed for infrastructure projects to result in success.

Responsible Growth in Financial Services

The catastrophic failures of risk management practices in several global banks during the financial collapse of 2008 gave us important lessons about the kind of transformation needed in large financial institutions.

The collapse of Lehman Brothers was a very serious and well-known case. Other examples across the sector in the United States and Europe are only slightly less extreme. The relentless pressure to grow revenues and profits at all costs was considerable at these institutions before the financial collapse. Certain senior leaders may have been culpable in leading once-great organizations into very dangerous waters. What these leaders did not foresee was a radically different external landscape that would completely upend their strategies and plans. The role of leaders in financial institutions has to be to provide responsible finance and achievement of sustainable growth. The entire sector is now relearning this. Citigroup, for example, is showing real seriousness in this regard.

Change-agile ways of thinking, doing, and being can help the transformation of financial services institutions so they connect head, heart, hands, and spirit. Attendance at leadership conferences or well-designed training events alone is not enough for leaders in financial institutions. The real process of transformation will only occur as they work together as enterprise leaders on collective problems toward a common purpose that goes beyond the numbers.

For Human Resource, Learning, and Organization Development Leaders: Designing Powerful Change Agility Leadership Programs

There is no right or wrong order in which to grow change capability, and there is no one-size-fits-all approach. Much depends on the lifecycle of a business. In general, we have found that the key is to connect the development of individual leaders with the development of the wider organization rather than treat them as separate activities.

It seems common in today's organizations for HR functions to split the leadership development or talent function from the organization development function, with one focused on individual leaders and the other on the health of the overall organization. This can at times create competing agendas—when actually, these functions should be totally aligned.

In the model below, we link individual leader development with team development and organization development.

Growing Executive, Team and Enterprise Level Change Agility

Our holistic leadership and organization development methodology involves 3 building blocks - **Personal, Relational and Systemic**

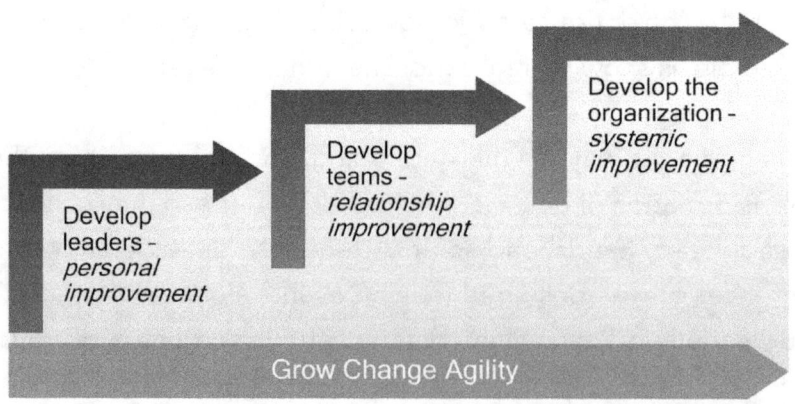

We see these as inseparable building blocks of change, moving from personal to relational and then to systemic improvement. One public service organization we work with has reintegrated its leadership and organization development arms after years of separation. This is entirely because of its growing appreciation that enterprise transformation can only occur if leaders are developed through experiences that occur in context, not purely in classrooms.

It is very natural and common for leaders (and those who help them from within the HR function or externally) to assume that the core skills needed in times of change are influencing without authority, engaging and aligning stakeholders, and other related communication skills. These still have weight as core skills for the effective leadership of change. However, what we have found is that change in an organization essentially takes place through adult dialogue rather than through any one party influencing another. Skills that relate to effective conversations really turn very generic development relating to change management into more specific development relating to transformative conversations which relate directly to a collective enterprise context.

There is a profoundly important link between the appropriate orchestration and management of conversations and change agility. Conversations needed in times of change are often delayed or are held in a way that does not allow new perspectives and realities to emerge. Alternatively, conversations during times of change can become too confrontational or focused on the wrong priorities. In general, it is simply worth the time and the effort to think through what conversations are needed at which levels, among which groups of staff, or between which individuals to create a climate for change. A big element of change agility, therefore, is planning these conversations and handling them so that the outcomes are productive.

The approach we encourage you to adopt for better connection between leadership and organization development during times of change is "conversation architecture." This approach anchors the whole process of change in needed, critical conversations. The diagram below illustrates how conversation architecture connects individual leadership with business-critical challenges. These are real-world challenges faced by the organization that leaders need to address as part of the process of transformational change. These are not the made-up or risk-free projects typical of many learning-and-development-driven "action learning" exercises. Rather, these challenges are genuinely mission critical to the business and *contain* cultural moments of truth.

Conversation Architecture - Creating Change Agility

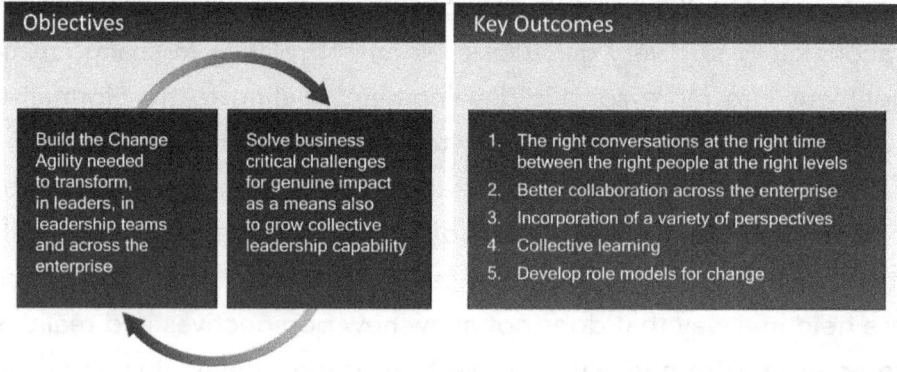

Objectives		Key Outcomes
Build the Change Agility needed to transform, in leaders, in leadership teams and across the enterprise	Solve business critical challenges for genuine impact as a means also to grow collective leadership capability	1. The right conversations at the right time between the right people at the right levels 2. Better collaboration across the enterprise 3. Incorporation of a variety of perspectives 4. Collective learning 5. Develop role models for change

Our experience is that the development of change agility occurs through collaboratively working on business-critical challenges in real time and during critical conversations. This method *connects* conversations with real-world challenges, which are associated both with leadership development and with enterprise transformation.

Through several years of designing and delivering leadership development programs and long-term change in large organizations, we have found that sustained changes in behavior occur when we combine deep personal reflection with real-world challenges. Nowadays, some kind of "project work" for leaders to undertake is a regular feature of leadership development programs so that they can apply some of the concepts they learn in the classroom or training room. While this is healthy, we don't believe this approach goes far enough to connect leadership development to the transformational change issues faced back at work after a program.

To improve on this, we have adopted a model for growing change agility that combines the best of different approaches in the leadership and organization development disciplines. The change-agile approach to development shifts the emphasis away from one purely on individual leaders themselves and toward the growth of enterprise-wide capability that supports transformation. Clearly, the individual is a critical focal point for the development of agility. However, our view is that leadership, rather than a set of leaders, is at the heart of change. Leadership is a process and an organizational experience borne out of relationships. IBM, for example, has been well known for transforming its change capability. Some years ago IBM undertook a major, global cultural transformation using this method, anchored in real-world problems which were connected to its own corporate values.

In this model of development, the role that external or internal facilitation plays is to help shape the process of behavioral change across the leadership team and the wider organization. Participants' feedback is unlikely to reveal too much about their actual behavior following learning events. The real evaluation that is needed is around collective outcomes, not participants' personal brief experiences of a facilitator. You can see below how we characterize this shift in emphasis from training events and their effect on individuals to the transformation of the whole human system.

Take an Agile Approach to Developing Leadership and Organization Effectiveness

Traditional Leadership Programs	The Agile Approach to Development
The individual is the target for personal learning	Individuals and relationships, within teams and organization systems, are targets for development
Learning occurs at off-site training events	Learning occurs where the issues are experienced and is enabled by facilitation
Tested through subsequent performance or behavior (if tested at all)	Effectiveness of learning indicated by business results and organizational health
May not be relevant to immediate problem. Learning focuses on theories and models of leadership	Real-life transformation issues shared by leaders across the business drive learning and self-reflection
Problems or case studies are designed and controlled by an external trainer	Problems are controlled by client, and solutions are designed with facilitation by a consultant

Evaluation criteria are defined by trainer and learning function. Usually measured by "happy sheet" scorecards	Evaluation criteria and the specific outcomes needed from change are determined by the business

In accelerated solutions workshops, leaders come together to debate issues, create collective clarity, and engage in constructive dialogue to generate solutions in an informal way. Solutions workshops are fundamentally different from traditional leadership programs. The outcome of some generic skills-training programs is a brief spike in personal awareness, and perhaps some people will come away with "key take-aways." Lasting organizational change, though, can only occur with continuous reinforcement of the right behavior in the context of real work. The focus of accelerated solutions events is to encourage joint problem solving and the critical conversations we described earlier.

Much executive learning in the area of change leadership stops at teaching executives about models for change and how they can personally adopt different behaviors rather than actually stimulating measurable shifts in actual performance. Agility acts as a conceptual and practical foundation to help leaders understand the kind of behavior expected of them and to explore their areas of strength and exposure. Our alternative approach to development that is tied into real-world problems is illustrated below.

Our aim here isn't to prescribe a specific formula for developing change agility. The model simply illustrates the need for a regular pulse of conversations about real-world issues and experiences that are also the subject of practical activity outside the classroom or workshop setting. The importance of teaching business-school style content becomes less important in this approach than actually making a difference to people who are working within an enterprise system and those whom the system seeks to serve. The whole process is a form of what psychologists call "action research"—applied to business-critical challenges.

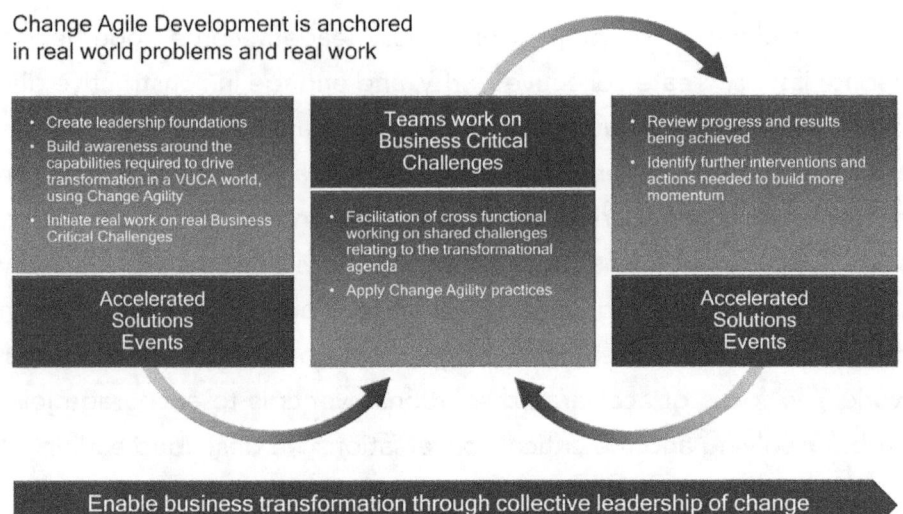

The diagram above illustrates an approach to development that combines leadership and organization development. Leaders are first given feedback, guidance, and coaching to ensure their alignment. Cross-functional teamwork on real-world business-critical challenges is initiated; facilitation and support are applied as needed. Leaders are encouraged to build their peer networks in this process and to break down internal silos to address the most serious dilemmas or sources of complexity for the organization. Further events are designed to create more change and more momentum around these challenges in the business rather than simply expose leaders to more theoretical models or frameworks.

We find that far too much leadership development is more or less divorced from the operational and strategic realities in the organization. We believe that executive development has been too focused on theoretical knowledge and loosely applicable personal insights and self-awareness instead of practical, systemic behavioral change and an application that impacts important moments of truth in the organization.

Attempts to build in some practicality tend to result in "action learning" projects that, in our experience, can have several unintended consequences. The biggest issue for many action-learning initiatives we see in organizations is that the projects are either unrealistic or are not supported from the outset by senior leadership. When learning occurs, it tends to happen on projects that are strongly sponsored from the outset and aligned to the needs of the organization. The work done within executive development has to be properly aligned to the business transformation agenda and must have very high levels of senior executive sponsorship.

To this end, we believe that business-critical challenges should be identified collectively across the business. The learning process includes not just identifying the challenges but also scoping the work needed to address them. Leaders then need to manage the change that puts solutions in place. This can only be done if the outcomes of the work to be done are measurable and material to the future success of the business, rather than "nice to have."

The other types of action-based (experiential) learning we come across regularly include forms of informal team building; brief, community-based projects; and also business simulations. When using community projects as a basis for learning try to be mindful that they are most effective when your business can have a direct impact on the community. In general, although these sorts of activities can have a strong place in executive learning, they can also often feel too far removed from everyday reality for learning to be transferable. It's like learning to play a concerto on a grand piano with a pair of chopsticks. The same thing can be said about some team building activities. An outdoor team building activity, whether it is clay pigeon shooting in the UK, dragon boat racing in Singapore, or a treasure hunt in the desert in Dubai, all need to be linked explicitly to the organization's espoused values, and its leadership philosophy, At the very least these events need to help executives actually surface the true nature of their relationships rather than simply have fun together in a temporarily politically sanitized environment.

In some corporate events we have observed and been asked to support, the elements of interest, novelty, brief suspension of internal politics, and even entertainment or theatrical 'wow' factor somehow seem to overshadow development rooted in measurable enterprise outcomes. Even in reputable business schools, certain professors and professional trainers are particularly adept at delivering high-quality "edutainment" for corporate clients, with questionable practical outcomes.

Our experience, too, is that any kind of external business simulation seems less powerful than the real thing: learning by doing, then reflecting on your experiences in your actual work. A temporary, simulated learning environment needs to help you deal better with the complexity of your realities, not dilute these realities for the sake of entertainment. While we understand that business simulation activities and outside-the-box team-building experiences do play a role in enabling organizational change, without the right design input from the business, these methods can actually detract from the complex business challenges corporate leaders face back in the office or in the field. Programs of any kind that companies create for their executives, if too disconnected from real business, run the risk of being seen as "nice to haves" rather than must-haves, and in the end they are just ways to avoid difficult but important conversations.

Development occurs when tough realities are brought into development experiences rather than left at work until after a program is over. When learning events are required parts of a program of change, events should be designed in context, not out of it. Clients should be given time and space to reflect on their own issues together and should feel that programs they attend support their business agendas. Of course, we believe that some time to detach oneself from day-to-day business, to reflect on one's own behavior, and to engage in learning new concepts or practices is helpful. The key point is that development practices can be even more powerful if programs create much better lines of sight to business challenges and outcomes. We need to connect leadership and organization development initiatives first to each other and then to business realities much better than we often do.

Some criticism could also be leveled at many off-site team-building meetings. Executive time is precious. When we bring together large groups of senior people from multiple global locations, every moment should really be spent engaging in real, honest conversations, no matter how tough they have to be. Some organizations, however, spend a large chunk of their off-site time giving high-level update presentations to attendees that could have been done via videoconference. Or they have quite generic discussions about their leadership challenges without engaging deeply enough in the specifics.

Such low-confrontation work might be done with a typical coach facilitating the meeting to offer fairly lighthearted even superficial exploration of leadership behavior. Many generic facilitators, coaches, or trainers without deeper organization development skills are actually not equipped to help leaders to have more honest and practical conversations about the things that get in the way of their performance or their ability to change. A good facilitator helps clients to "put the moose on the table" or address the "elephant in the room" constructively. Leadership events that are only entertaining and psychologically very safe are unlikely to be game-changing meetings. Some executives in such programs are actually unlikely to raise difficult or sensitive issues if they feel it would spoil the artificially harmonious, compliant atmosphere or create political exposure. A fine balance needs to be struck between fun, celebration of success, reenergizing people in a general sense, and a bit of authentic and honest scrutiny of actual relationships. We find that too much executive development and especially team building activity is becoming dominated by games and gimmicks that detract from the enriched awareness of self and others. Additionally, few facilitators have the skills or the courage to help groups go beyond the false harmony and fake camaraderie that is so present in many corporate gatherings, both large and small.

We do believe that many executives go along to off-site corporate team-building events and to leadership programs knowing that the process is required to show their commitment, to keep HR happy, and to show face to the CEO or department head sponsoring the meeting. They tend to go with the flow, which is heavily stage-managed. However, good facilitation can help groups to surface and address their collective challenges fruitfully—and to go deeper into their issues, if necessary. Poor facilitation simply skates across the surface, but it feels good, like a nice, warm bath. This is particularly true if participants are returning to a toxic or dysfunctional workplace after an event. As a client recently said to me, you can take a goldfish out of a bowl of dirty water and put it in some clean water for a while, but unless you clean the bowl, the fish will go back to a dirty environment. More leadership development efforts actually need to address the health of both the fish and the water at the same time – which is challenging to achieve in practice.

Perhaps the weakest part of any extended executive team-building or formal development program is in the final few hours. In this final stage, executives are nearly always asked to consolidate their learning and think about their personal actions. Our fear is that, more often than not, personal action plans from leadership development or team-building events are poor quality, not very specific, and frequently simply shelved along with the binder of glossy handouts or notes that were taken until the following year's event. The best way to make action plans stick is to translate personal insight into subsequent action on real business-critical challenges, perhaps captured in a written and collective leadership charter. By linking insight to action that relates to work life and then to business outcomes, we can reinforce the spiral of value. Personal insight needs stronger links to the creation of enterprise value and enablement of transformation.

Much individual executive coaching also fails to make this connection because it is done out of context. In some organizations, executive coaching has taken root so strongly that is offered to all of the top executives almost as a perk or badge of appreciation and support. However, it is targeted purely at individuals for their own personal development and is so highly individualized that its value seems impossible to track. The coaching method used in some companies seems to lack the setting of any kind of mutual expectation, structure, or focal points related to broader organizational priorities. Some facilitation, training, and coaching methods appear to lack any serious connection to a firm's business or strategic agenda. The field of coaching is also unfortunately very open to consultants without the right knowledge, depth, critical thinking ability, background, or professional credentials. There are a multitude of coach accreditation bodies of varying rigor, most of which are not statutory or subject to real regulatory oversight. Some of the bodies that train, accredit, and supervise the practice of training and coaching have the sole purpose to grow their own membership and services rather than demonstrably to help the recipients of coaching.

The barriers to entry in the coaching and training industry are, in our experience, extremely low…so buyer, beware. We have seen many examples of consultancies of various kinds overpromising and under-delivering when it comes to supporting organization change with the quality of their tools and their people. Organizations often do need external help to build the cultural norms that reinforce the values of the firm as a whole, though. Our perspective is that large companies that hire professionals to help with the complex human challenges of change should require consultants to provide firmer evidence of their actual professional credentials.

Selecting appropriate external partners for change is not simply hiring an astute consultant or "executive coach" who has struck up a friendship with the CEO. Such an act creates tension and credibility issues when the coach starts to play a bigger role in the wider organization, which is common. In the United Kingdom, chartered occupational psychologists working independently as organization development and change practitioners go through a minimum of seven years of academic and on-the-job, supervised training in accredited institutions before working unsupervised with clients. Similar regulatory standards apply to practitioners of industrial and organizational psychology in several parts of the world. The fact is, however, that clients can and do choose to work with celebrity coaches or consultants who are good at selling their ideas and especially performing "in the room" with them in large events, somewhat akin to celebrity magicians, regardless of their actual qualifications or depth of robust knowledge and know-how about behavioral change.

A properly qualified professional who has a written code of ethics has your interests at heart. Professionalism in people development requires honesty about the *limitations* of the tools available and is as targeted and evidence based as possible. Businesses and public sector organizations need to choose external partners for major change efforts carefully. Organizations could easily benefit from being more discerning and more selective in their use of experts to reduce the growing cynicism about change within their workforce. A good consultant in the area of organizational change is genuinely interested in your people, in your human and business realities, helps you craft your own internal change capability, and helps your leaders improve their collective impact.

There are plenty of opportunities to be creative in how we encourage shifts. We can foster deeper purpose in the context of experiences and conversations derived directly from the business you are actually in and from its various stakeholders. The hard work of strategy execution has the biggest learning impact, differentiates the agile from the less agile, and creates lasting change. When you find your results improving and that the transformation you want is occurring, it can be deeply satisfying. There is plenty of psychological evidence showing that you can act yourself into new ways of thinking, not just try to think yourself into new ways of acting. The nature of agile development is that it is rooted in the here and now, in reflection, action, experimentation and evidence of the resulting outcomes.

Call to Action: Grow Change Agility in HR First

Global and Regional HR Transformation: We have encountered numerous client attempts to restructure and transform HR functions, both globally and in different regions of the world. The emphasis of these efforts tends to be to reposition HR as a "strategic partner" to the business—to lead the business and support business change—rather than be an operational support function handling HR processes and procedures. While this is a caricatured description of many HR transformation initiatives, it is the essence of many.

Part of the interest in these initiatives is often also wrapped up in reducing HR operational costs through leaner, shared services capabilities, outsourcing, and technology platforms of various descriptions (both specific, specialist, point solutions for areas such as talent management and broader, employee self-service "e-HR" systems).

HR functions often house the learning and development function and also frequently an organization development and talent function. One of these is likely also to handle leadership development. There is usually a separate compensation specialist team in HR advising on rewards issues. Frequently, there is also an employee relations team in a further specialist unit. On the whole, HR structures, given multiple assignments as "centers of excellence," global and regional business partners, and shared services, can be confusing and difficult for leaders and employees to navigate. The challenges for HR, whatever its structure, are credibility and business value. These are addressed partly with more agile, streamlined HR operating models. HR leaders across the board also need to demonstrate their own change agility as leaders.

Change-Agile HR Leadership

Our research and experience of HR functions tell us that HR can and should play an essential role in building more change-capable businesses that are equipped to thrive in a VUCA world. However, there is often a gap in adequate change agility in HR itself. This can be particularly true in markets where HR functions have less experience in leading and managing large-scale change in the business.

One of the key development priorities for HR leaders and their teams, especially in transforming regions like Asia and the Middle East, is to develop change leadership skills in themselves and in their HR business partner teams. The business partners tend to be those working most closely with the business day to day. They support line leaders through periods of change or transformation. For them to do this, they need sophisticated facilitation, consulting, and change delivery skills, not a purely technical, process-oriented or policy-focused HR skill set. The required skills need a great deal of practice and dedicated development support using robust methods.

How Can HR Leaders Develop Change-Agile HR to Support Change Agility in the Business?

Our perspective is that HR leaders should align HR functional skill and capability development to the leadership and management of change in the business. Once HR is ready and equipped to drive change, business leaders are more likely to feel that they also need to be active change agents.

It is vital that HR leaders stay a step ahead of the change curve by showing that their own team is agile and responsive to business needs and to change.

THREE KEY IDEAS TO TAKE AWAY FROM THIS SECTION

1   The place to start the development of change agility is *you*. Have the courage to seek feedback from those you work with on your ability to lead change and to cope with the pace of change. Use this feedback to adjust your behavior and style.

2   The second place to focus is on your team, either the one you lead, the one you are in, or both. Create a team that is ready for change, able to respond to opportunity, and equipped to manage risk in a VUCA world. A high-performance team is agile by design.

3   Finally, the overall organizational context really counts toward change agility. Play your part in the development of a winning culture by helping others to embrace change. Find out what the drivers for change are in your organization. Put together your own strategy for agility.

There is nothing so difficult or so dangerous as to
undertake to change the order of things.

—Niccolò Machiavelli

Uncertainty requires us to act ourselves into new ways of thinking as well as to think ourselves into new ways of acting.

Develop Senior Leaders and Executives in Support of Successful Transformational Change

Change agility is a model for building greater understanding and awareness around the leadership needed in your organization during times of change. The change leadership archetypes and some reflection on how they apply to our own styles are helpful in this regard. We have applied many existing and well-tested models, all covering differing aspects of change and of leadership, to establish the various elements of change agility, including the seven cultural orientations and the leadership dilemmas.

A group of senior executives who are leading a strategic initiative or playing a broad leadership role may well benefit from open discussions about their personal preferences and the sources of strength they can provide to the process of transformation. Given the complex and sometimes chaotic nature of organizational change, some personal reflection will help grow a stronger appreciation of the strengths one can bring to bear to deal with complexity. Every leader has something to offer, and most leadership teams include a mix of individual strengths and capabilities.

Change leadership capabilities must start with the senior leaders in every organization, particularly the top executive team, because that is where an enterprise sets the tone for the culture. Whether you choose specifically to apply the model provided in this guidebook exactly as we have described it is actually less important than making the growth of change capability a business priority and that you see change as requiring a better method than the classical top-down or simple, project-managed approach.

How You Can Use Change Agility to Thrive in a VUCA World

Although we have been repeating and reinforcing the same central messages throughout this guide—that in today's world, you will benefit from the ability to create adaptive personal and organizational change capabilities—we also assume that other things also influence your success. Clearly, circumstances play a very significant role. Purely good or bad luck can change and turn in an instant in an executive career—and for a whole organization. However, research shows that chance favors the prepared leader and organization.

Change agility provides you with a model for change and for personal leadership that can help you choose your response in difficult situations rather than simply react. It is an approach that draws on several different disciplines and sources, a synthesis of what we believe counts in the world all of us are now in.

You can choose to apply change agility in any of three ways:

- Build your own self-awareness around areas where you are naturally proficient and areas that might leave you exposed. Are you, for example, great at creating a sense of direction and aspiration for yourself and for others, but less strong at generating momentum that accelerates into the future?

- Help your team grow individual and collective proficiency at change. Being able to cope with and implement changes in one's work and one's life are crucial to personal effectiveness now. In an era in which the very notion of a career is being redefined, we all can benefit from learning what it takes to be good at change.

- Use different aspects of the approach we have described to inform the development of a winning organization if you are an enterprise leader or an HR leader. Change agility operates at all levels—individual, team, and enterprise. Managing considerable complexity at the top executive level requires certain skills and capabilities, which we have outlined. It is worth reflecting, perhaps, on whether these capabilities are present in your organization—and if not, what that might mean for you and your colleagues.

When the winds of change blow, some people build walls and others build windmills.

—Chinese proverb

Parting thoughts: Use This Book to Inform the Way You Lead and Manage Change in Your Organization

Organizational change is often complex and high risk. Our hope in creating our guide has been that its approach will complement your existing understanding of change leadership and change management. There are many approaches to choose from, and we often work with other models for organizational change with our clients. Our view is that there are several models of behavioral change that can help improve the results you get from large-scale transformation or from strategy execution.

We don't propose for a second that the specific combination of success factors or language we have used in this guide are the right or best to use at all times in all situations for all organizations or leaders. However, the key elements of change agility, some of its underlying premises, reflect academic research as well as personal learning, thought, and experience. In a rapidly evolving global economic, technological, political, climactic, and regulatory landscape, the discipline of change itself needs to evolve. We think that if you can take just one or two of the ideas we have put forward and make your own organization more change ready and more change capable, then we have succeeded.

Agility is the defining attribute of high-performance organizations in this era. We have attempted to articulate what this looks like in practice at the individual, team, and enterprise levels and to provide some guidance on what you can do to move in the right direction.

We wish you luck with your leadership and change journey.

Cross the river by feeling the stones.

—Chinese proverb

THREE CONTINUAL STEPS FOR YOUR GROWTH

Reflect

Reflect on your preferences around change. What are your strengths? What do you tend to contribute to changes in the organization, and how do you help to achieve organizational renewal? We each contribute to change in different ways.

Relate

Relate your experiences of change and your own reflections to other people's experiences and reflections. Discuss them openly to calibrate your own practice with other leaders in the organization. Relate this also to your team's experiences of you.

Reinforce

Reinforce the behavioral changes you would like to make for yourself, your team, and your organization. Try to identify the key areas where you feel progress can be made, and then hold yourself to account. Tell others what you plan to do differently so they can help you just try things out.

This is a virtuous cycle in which you constantly do all of these things to achieve personal growth as a leader of change.

Your Turn: Three Personal Insights

You Have Generated About Your Ability to Manage

Uncertainty and to Harness Change

Personal
Insight 1

Personal
Insight 2

Personal
Insight 3

If you have built castles in the air, your work

need not be lost; that is where they should be.

Now put the foundations under them.

—Henry David Thoreau

ABOUT THE AUTHOR

Kiran Chitta
MA (Oxon), MSc, CPsychol, AFBPsS

Kiran Chitta is an organizational psychologist with twenty years of experience in the study and transformation of human performance. Kiran has held executive positions in both mature and emerging markets for blue-chip, multinational corporations including Procter & Gamble and Motorola. He has been a member of the British Senior Civil Service, facilitating UK central government transformation. He has held senior human capital advisory roles in global consulting firms including Oliver Wyman, Deloitte, and Accenture. He works as an enabler of change internationally in several sectors including financial services, consumer goods and retail, telecom, media, technology, professional services, travel, hospitality, health care, and government. Kiran has a degree in experimental psychology from the University of Oxford and a master's with distinction in organizational psychology from the University of Manchester Institute for Science and Technology. He is a UK chartered occupational psychologist and an associate fellow of the British Psychological Society.

www.ingramcontent.com/pod-product-compliance
Lightning Source LLC
Chambersburg PA
CBHW051639170526
45167CB00001B/253